02

Horses of the World

BOOKS BY THE SAME AUTHOR
Successful Show Jumping, 1951; 2nd edition, 1962
Know Your Pony, 1955
Huntsmen of a Golden Age, 1956
Silver Spring, 1958
Die Pferde mit der Elchschaufel, 1960; 2nd edition, 1963
The Foals of Epona, with A. A. Dent, 1962
British Native Ponies, 1963

TRANSLATION
The Noble Horse, 1963

Horses of the World

An Illustrated Survey, with over 320 Photographs
of Breeds of Horses and Ponies

DAPHNE MACHIN GOODALL

PREFACE BY C. W. ANDERSON

Foreword by The Duke of Beaufort, K.G., G.C.V.O., M.F.H.

THE MACMILLAN COMPANY
NEW YORK

CONTENTS

5

10247

ACKNOWLEDGMENTS

The author gratefully acknowledges the help given by H.R.H. Prince Ludwig of Bavaria, Frau Zapp (wife of the German Ambassador to Venezuela), Mrs de Fries, Baroness von Langenn, the Breed Societies, the Press Attachés and Public Relations Officers of Embassies, and many others who very kindly provided photographs or information: Abernathy Photo Co.; American Embassy; American Quarter Horse Association; American Saddle Horse Breeders Association; American Shetland Pony Club; Einar Andersson; Sr. D'Andrade; Appaloosa Horse Club; Sr. Arata; Australian News and Information Bureau; J. R. Bainbridge; Barnabys; C. T. Blackwood; British Council, Lima; Robert Brislawn; Canadian Geographical Journal; Canada House; Chronicle of the Horse; Cie des Arts Photomechaniques; Harold W. Cline; F. G. Dawson; Professor S. Dyrendahl; Editions S.E.P.T.; Egyptian State Tourist Office; Oscar Ehlert; M. Filimonov; Elsbeth Geiger; T. Gil; E. Gobert; Greek Embassy; G. Halling Nielsen; Directeur des Haras; Mabel Harford; The Harness Horse; Vare Hester; P. Russell Howell; Iceland Tourist Information Bureau; Iowa Palomino Exhibitors Association Inc.; Iranian Embassy; Institute of Horse Breeding; International Press Agency; Valok K. Lahdenniemi; Lantbruksfilm; Libyan Embassy; J. H. M. Lindeman; Captain O. J. M. Lindsay; Cornelius Linfert; S. W. Lock; Machatschek; Mariani; Meteor; Missouri Fox Trotting Horse Breed Association; John Nestle; Norwegian Embassy; V. Noskov; Palomino Horse Breeders of America; John W. Patten; Pinto Horse Association of America Inc.; Pony of the Americas Club Inc.; Paul Popper; Portuguese Embassy; Dr. W. Pruski; Froeken Ingrid Roing; General Santa Rosa; Michal Rudowski; Ruth Seering; Erika Schiele; M. Skronski; Society for Cultural Relations with the U.S.S.R.; Sovfoto; Spanish Embassy; Sport & General; H. Sting; Stud Book de la Race Ardennais; Tass; Tennessee Walking Horse Breeders' and Exhibitors' Association of America; Tiedemann; Uitgeverij Ploegsma; H. Veenman & Zonen; L. Velikzhanin; Virginian Department of Conservation and Economic Development; Maureen Walton; Guido Wedding; Welsh Pony Society of America; White Horse Ranch.

PREFACE

A glance at the title of this book would make it seem a monumental undertaking; a study of its contents proves that this is truly so. But it is also so obviously a labor of love that any hint of the toil involved has vanished in the enthusiasm of the undertaking.

A more complete book on horses would be hard to find. The most remote breeds and strains have been searched out; excellent pictures are shown of all of them, and all the known facts are given. That fine turf writer, the late Joe Palmer, gave as his credo, 'A fact and an opinion are not the same and that distinction should always be made.' This the author of *Horses of the World* has borne in mind throughout this informative book.

In planning this work it was clearly understood that no amount of description can convey the characteristics and qualities of a horse as well as a good picture. And the pictures, which appear on every page, are uniformly excellent, taken by one who knows the angle and view that best show the points of a horse without the distortion of foreshortening so obvious in pictures taken by a photographer who is not a horseman.

Even those who feel quite knowledgeable on the subject can learn a great deal from this book, particularly about the origin of the horse, with its beginnings so far in the dim past. Shown are pictures of horses from remote parts of the world, which are closest to the earliest members of the horse family, the Eohippus, and bear enough resemblance to make credible the relationship.

Also shown are the differences within breeds developed in different countries, with many types and strains that have never come to the attention of this reader in other books on the subject. Particularly admirable is the direct and concise way in which all information is given, with just enough color and incident to enhance the picture and add to the reading pleasure.

This book could well serve as a complete and authoritative encyclopedia of horses. A close study of it would be of interest to, and add considerably to the knowledge of, even a seasoned horseman. When one has finished it, he will truly be in the spirit of those old fox hunters in weathered scarlet when they raised high their glasses in that ancient toast, 'Gentlemen, the horse!'

C. W. ANDERSON

FOREWORD

By The Duke of Beaufort, K.G., G.C.V.O., M.F.H.

The interest taken in the horse increases yearly. There will be many, therefore, like myself, who will find in *Horses of the World* new breeds, of which little is known. Indeed the book includes many names of which I have never heard. The photographs, too, are numerous and extremely helpful in supporting Miss Machin Goodall's description of the various breeds.

I am happy, therefore, to write this short Foreword, and in it to thank Miss Machin Goodall for writing a book that will greatly increase both one's knowledge of horses of the world and one's interest in the horse.

COLOUR PLATES

MONOCHROME PLATES

EUROPE: WARM-BLOOD HORSES

12

INTRODUCTION

It gives me very great pleasure to present, in this book, my 'stable' of horses and ponies. Many of them have never before been collected together between the covers of one book; and a number of breeds and types were new to me, so that it was of tremendous interest to gather information about them.

It has been a fascinating process to discover the origins of some of these breeds, collected from the far corners of the earth. Indeed, I believe I may say that the reader will find that a number of 'discoveries' have been made; or at least there are details that have not commonly appeared in print. Some of these discoveries have their own mysteries still concealed.

I heard vaguely one day of some 'wild' horses on an island in the middle of the Atlantic! These wild horses turned out to be the ponies on Sable Island, off Nova Scotia, whose history as far as it is known will be found in the following pages. But the mystery remains: how did the ponies arrive on the island? Were they shipwrecked, or were a few brought there on purpose, for the use of the lighthousemen, and did they increase in their own good time? No one seems to know.

The ancestry of the Arab has produced another fascinating link. Contrary to the gospel spread by many pro-Arab people, the Arabian horse is not a species unto itself; it evolved just the same as did every other breed, since evolution is a process that has been going on since the dawn of time. But from what type of horse did the Arabian evolve? One begins with the fact, and fact it is indeed, that there were few horses in Arabia and those only in the coastal areas, until the Prophet Mohammed saw fit to mount his armies. Before there were Arabian horses in Arabia, there were Oriental horses in Turkey, Persia, Syria and Turkmen. The Turkmene horses were noted for their speed and were used as racehorses around 1,000 B.C. And the odd thing is that the Turkmene horse bears a very distinct likeness to the Munighi Arabian, who helped to found the Thoroughbred! In the 18th century many Munighi Arabians and so-called Barbs were not shipped to Britain from Arabia but from Aleppo in Syria. It is worth while to compare the photographs of the Turkmene, Achal-Teké, Persian Arab, Jaf and Tchenerani with the Arabians of Europe, and to consider all these in a possible relationship with the Thoroughbred.

With the exception of the Thoroughbred, all these breeds are hundreds of years old, whilst the latter is a very new young breed; at the most it is scarcely two hundred and fifty years old.

13

Of all the breeds all over the world, the breeding of the Thoroughbred has become an industry, with the complicated machinery needed to run an industry. Should the eye of the master no longer look with love on his horse but instead to his increasing bank balance, then, as is the way with all things that are not loved, it may be in danger of disappearing. Although the Thoroughbred has found a home in many countries, it is already a fact that, in some of them, the breed degenerates very quickly unless additions of new blood are imported from England. So the Thoroughbred is not entirely a fixed breed.

Perhaps we have a case for introducing some 'old' blood and founding new lines? We certainly have a case for examining the desirability of such action and for ensuring that the qualities of stamina and hardiness are not lost in this breed. For these qualities are needed wherever Thoroughbred blood is used to 'improve' other breeds, and although it may well have been a benefit a hundred years ago, can the same be said today?

Perhaps these pictures have made us aware, too, of that other pure-bred racehorse —the Trotter. The Trotter has just as much blue blood in his veins as any other fashionable breed; and generally he can trace his pedigree back farther than many of his human contemporaries. What the Trotter lacks in honour from the conservative worshippers of the Thoroughbred, he makes up in endurance. And his excesses of endurance must delight his fans. His popularity is increasing and recently two new breeds have emerged—the Noram, the French racing Trotter; and the Métis, the new Russian Trotter.

Another discovery that we have made is of the presence of the Ice Age horse— *Equus przevalskii przevalskii* Poljakoff—in our midst. These horses are to be found in the Zoos of Whipsnade, Catskill, Washington, Chicago, Rotterdam, Amsterdam, Antwerp, Münich-Hellabrun, Berlin, Copenhagen, Paris, Askania Nova and in Prague, which has the biggest herd of all. And they are not, as some would have us believe, a cross with a Mongolian pony. It is, however, a sad reflection on the human race that, quite probably, in their last natural stronghold in the Gobi Desert, the wild horse of Mongolia has been hunted out of existence during recent months.

As we turn the pages of this book, one thing makes itself abundantly clear; in every respect, right down to our day, the age of the atom bomb, mechanisation and industrialisation, the horse has fulfilled his destiny to serve. Just as, from the dawn of history, when man owed his culture and his progress to his association with the horse, so today there are peoples whose existence still depends upon the help given them by their horses or ponies.

It would be a good thing if we paused for a moment to consider what life would be like if there were no horses. Shall we allow them to disappear?

In this book there are photographs of young horses, of ponies and of foals, and that foals continue to make their appearance is due to the affection and the sacrifice which breeders are willing to make. Generally speaking, foals do not 'just happen' any more. Man has taken control of that and he can up-grade or down-grade the equine species as the whim takes him. Those breeders who continue to allow the laws of nature to operate, who insist on breeding true, instead of following some fashionable fancy, are those to whom future generations may give thanks.

If horses and ponies are to remain with us, if future generations of mankind are to know the blessings which association with horses bestows on them, then it is to these breeders—the directors of the big studs and the 'little' men and women—to whom we should be ever grateful. For it is they, together with the men who grow the food, who are keeping alive a great heritage.

This book is an illustrated survey of the breeds of horse and pony that exist in the world today. 'Illustrated' is the important word, for my main purpose has been to collect together as good pictures as possible of every breed that has been photographed. If any breed is omitted or if any country is not represented—as for example some of the South American states—it is either because photographs were quite unobtainable or because the types of South American Criollo, Llanero or Prairie horses are so much alike whatever their country.

The captions under the photographs are as full as possible, and for each breed there is a summary of its locality, characteristics, colours, height and so on in concise form—a handy breed index.

The introductory text is subsidiary to the illustrations. Although horses know nothing of boundaries or frontiers and will flourish just as well in one country as another, provided they are cared for, it has been found necessary for the sake of convenience to divide the text into continents and sub-divide it into countries. Readers, however, will realize that certain breeds—Arabs, for instance, or Thoroughbreds—are found in many different countries, although they are described under their country of origin.

There are no national divisions drawn in this book, because horses have no political interest whatever in those countries where they are destined to live; and the breeders of horses all over the world are probably the least politically-minded of the human species.

The order of placing the breeds in the text has been done to give the reader a better idea of the *effect* of a certain breed on neighbouring breeds. For this reason the text begins with the Tarpan of Poland (Europe), because the Tarpan—*Equus przevalskii gmelini* Antonius—was a wild species of considerable numbers and its territory extended from the Caucasus throughout Western Europe. Tarpan blood, therefore, was the basis of many Oriental and primitive pony breeds and through them to later-day warm-blood horses and subsequently Thoroughbreds. One of the oldest European warm-blood breeds to influence others is the East Prussian horse of Germany, so Germany follows Poland and so on.

15

In the same way *Equus przevalskii przevalskii* Poljakoff, the Mongolian wild horse, receives pride of place under the heading of Asia.

It was a task of some magnitude to collect photographs and information of so many breeds and types of horses and ponies, and although the greatest care has been taken to be accurate and many authorities consulted—some of whom differed—apologies are here made for any inadvertent mistakes; to err is human.

The ancestors of the horse have been dealt with very briefly, for pre-history is outside the scope of this book, which is concerned with modern breeds as the illustrations show. If the interest of readers is awakened so that they wish to delve into the early history, the bibliography should help them.

Henny, 1965.   D.M.G.

AND GOD CREATED THE HORSE...

When horses accepted the burden
Of treading narrow human paths
And took the royal oath to serve,
The angels whispered low together:
'Oh, that man learns from their charity,
Their courage, kindness and loyalty,
He shall learn that the love of horses
Is a language the wide world over,
Which knows no distinctions.
Let him learn that this,
This is one of God's noblest creatures'.

                                                                    D.M.G.

16

ENVIRONMENT, DISTRIBUTION AND DEVELOPMENT

In some degree every living creature, including man, is related to the horse. Millions of years ago they shared the same ancestors. 'The same fishes, the same amphibians, the same reptiles, and the same early mammals were destined to give rise to both horses and men. We are blood relatives of the horse, and rather close relatives when the whole of the animal kingdom is compared'.*

No other living creature has had the same cultural effect upon civilizations of man or has so helped him to achieve his ambitions; and in many ways no other creature has suffered as much as the horse has at the hands of his blood relative.

Whether we choose to agree or disagree, results of the latest scientific collaboration between biologists, zoologists and archaeologists point to a common ancestor for all breeds of horses from the middle and late Tertiary: *Equus przevalskii,* whose immediate descendant is *Equus przevalskii przevalskii* Poljakoff, or the Mongolian wild horse (p. 172).

Horses populated the world long before man evolved into a human being, and a considerable population it must have been too. Since the beginning of history (a fairly recent event) the numbers of horses which roamed the world so freely have decreased enormously until today when one breed after another is fast disappearing. Will the Nuclear Age prove to have caused the extinction of the species *equus?* It may, however, astonish the reader to discover just how great is the number of different breeds and types of horses and ponies to be found at the present time, scattered in many different countries throughout the world.

In fact horses continue to be bred in all the recognised continents—Europe, Asia, Africa, Australasia and North and South America. Many countries within these continents specialise in particular breeds which may be regarded as 'native', although perhaps not indigenous, to these countries. Sometimes these native breeds, like the *Arab,* whose ancestry lies in Persia, have established themselves so successfully in other lands that they have come to be regarded as belonging there.

* Dr. George Gaylord Simpson: *Horses.*

17

The *Thoroughbred,* although originating in England, has made a name and a home for himself all over the world. Not only that, the *Arab,* the *Thoroughbred* and the native pony of certain countries, when mated, have established *fixed* breeds of horses with all their own peculiarities and specialities.

Apart from the recognised breeds, there are many different types of horses and ponies. All these breeds and types serve the purpose for which man requires them, and they have adapted themselves to every condition of climate and service.

Breeds of horses must be studied in relationship to their environment. The chief factors which govern the distribution and development of the species *equus* are climate, soil, light, constitution of food and water and their accessibility or otherwise, and domestication which includes selective breeding in order to obtain animals for definite purposes.

The extremes of temperature in countries where the horse is found play an important part in developing his resistance; and his extraordinary ability to adapt himself to climatic changes is one of the most remarkable qualities which the horse possesses. For instance, generally speaking, ponies which are able to grow a thick coat are found in the colder northern climates and mountainous regions, while the hot climates have produced a noble, elegant animal with a thin skin and fine coat—the hot-blood horse. Damp climates (producing lush grazing) have produced the slow, heavy, cold-blood horse. In tropical climates is found a small, hard, energetic horse often of not particularly good conformation, but capable of enduring considerable hardship.

When we refer to 'blood'—cold-blood, for example—it has nothing to do with blood temperature; the term is used to express the amount of *Thoroughbred* or *Arab* blood, or lack of it, in the horse's pedigree; temperament, too, comes into it. A warm-blood horse has neither the 'fire' of the *Arab* or *Thoroughbred,* nor the cold, slow temperament of the heavy draught horse.

The *Shetland* pony, the *Shire* horse and the *Thoroughbred* are extremes in breeding and illustrate the differences of three distinct breeds.

The *Arab* and *Thoroughbred*—'*Pur sang*' or '*Vollblut*'—are regarded as the noblest and most excellent of the species, and breeding has been developed upon the most scientific lines. Warm-blood horses are those whose ancestry contains the blood of the *Thoroughbred* and Oriental breeds, such as the *Arab, Barb* and *Turk,* and they are the native horses of certain European and American countries.

Cold-blood horses are derived from the heavy pre-historic horse of central Europe. Again environment played its part, for these animals roamed rich marshlands and developed passive qualities. They are different from the *Shetland* pony, which is considered by some authorities to belong to the cold-blood group, and which owes its diminutive size to the fact that it was a native of rocky islands with sparse grazing except during the month of June, and hard, cold winters.

Half-bred horses are usually crosses between heavy horses or native ponies and

Thoroughbreds, although in many cases the term is used to imply horses of unknown ancestry. *Anglo-Arab* and *Anglo-Norman* are the offspring of the cross between the *Thoroughbred* and the *Arab,* or the *Norman* horse. A country-bred horse is not a breed but a type common to a certain locality. Native ponies may be regarded (to facilitate terms of specification) as indigenous breeds, although all living horses today had their origin in Asia. There are, indeed, many so-called indigenous breeds of horses and ponies which have occupied certain territories for several thousands of years.

The expression 'wild' is an erroneous description for once-domesticated horses which are free to roam in herds and graze certain districts; the only true wild horses left in the world today are the Mongolian wild horses, whose native land for hundreds of thousands of years has been the steppe lands of the western Gobi desert. Undoubtedly this species could have been found, at one time, in many parts of Asia and Europe. Perhaps, too, the *Tarpan* (see p. 39) may be considered a wild animal— certainly its forebears in the not very distant past were wild and were classified as game. As such, in the Middle Ages, they were hunted for their meat and were regarded in eastern Europe as being quite useless for any other purpose.

If the following pages are studied carefully it will be seen how some breeds have been crossed to obtain other breeds. The original *Thoroughbred,* bred in England, possesses the blood of 'our mares' descending in part from local native ponies. The *Thoroughbred* has been exported all over the world and has improved many warm-blood breeds. For instance, the *Norfolk Roadster,* part-parent of the modern *Hackney,* together with the *Harddraver* of Holland, was exported to the United States and founded the *American Trotter,* which in turn returned to Europe to improve almost all trotting (racing) lines. The *Spanish* horses, taken there by Hernán Cortés, populated both North and South America and, together with other importations, thus formed the basis for all other breeds in the New World, as well as influencing practically all European breeds and some Russian breeds of horses. From pre-historic times the Oriental horse has found its way both east and west; and, long before the *Arabian* was known as such, was established in a number of recognised breeds.

It is natural enough that countries, districts or studs should give their name to a particular breed, but certain stallions have also founded breeds; these include Nonius, Furioso-North Star and Morgan. Some types of horses are called after their colour— Palomino and Albino, for example.

EUROPE: Warm-Blood Horses

POLAND. Tarpan *(Equus przevalskii gmelini* Ant.); Konik; Huzul; Sokólsk; Masuren; Poznan; Polish Arab; Polish Anglo-Arab.

GERMANY. Dülmen; Trakehner; Hanoverian; Oldenburg; Württemberg; German Arab.

HUNGARY. Nonius; Furioso; Lipizzaner; Shagya Arabian.

SPAIN. Sorraia; Andalusian; Carthusian; Spanish Arab.

PORTUGAL. Lusitano.

CZECHOSLOVAKIA. Kladruber.

AUSTRIA. Lipizzaner; Haflinger.

YUGOSLAVIA. Lipizzaner.

ITALY. Salerno; Calabrese; Avelignese.

FRANCE. French Thoroughbred; Demi-Sang Trotter; Noram Trotter; Norman; Camargue Pony; French Anglo-Arab.

SWITZERLAND. Freiberger; Einsiedler; Swiss Anglo-Norman; Swiss Holstein.

BELGIUM. Belgian Warm-Blood.

HOLLAND. Friesian; Gelderland; Groningen.

DENMARK. Fjord; Frederiksborg; Knabstrup.

SWEDEN. Gotland ('Skogsruss'); Swedish Warm-Blood.

NORWAY. Fjord (Fjording); Northlands; Döle-Gudbrandsdal; Döle Trotter.

GREECE. Peneia Pony; Pindos Pony; Skyros Pony.

ICELAND. Iceland Pony.

U.S.S.R. Viatka; Pechora (Zemaituka); Toric; Latvian; Lithuanian; Don; Kustanair; Budjonny; Kirghiz; Karabakh; Karabair; Kabardin; Lokai; Jomud; Achal-Teké; Turkmene; Strelets Arab; Orlov Trotter; Russian-American Trotter; Métis Trotter.

GREAT BRITAIN. Exmoor; New Forest; Dartmoor; Fell; Dales; Welsh Mountain; Welsh Pony; Welsh Cob; Highland; Shetland; Thoroughbred; Cleveland Bay; Hackney Horse; Hackney Pony; Spotted Horse.

REPUBLIC OF IRELAND. Connemara; Irish Hunter; Irish Cob.

21

E U R O P E: Warm-Blood Horses

With the exception of Australia, Europe is the smallest of the continents. Its boundaries to the west and north are the Atlantic Ocean and the Arctic Ocean, on the south the Mediterranean Sea, Black Sea and Caucasus, the eastern boundaries being the Caspian Sea, the Ural river and Ural mountains. The surface is divided into two parts—the great central plain stretching from the Ural mountains to the Atlantic and the highlands in the centre and south. The northern Scandinavian countries, Iceland and Scotland are extremely mountainous.

The climate of Europe is very diverse, varying from extreme cold in the east during the winter, hot summers in central and southern Europe where the latter also has a mild winter, to the mild, wet winters of the north-west regions. Although seasons and methods of agriculture vary on the great plain from the east to the west, much the same crops are grown, from the great corn-growing area of the Ukraine to the similar but smaller areas towards the west. The countries bordering the Baltic, having extremely cold winters and short, hot summers, are rye-growing areas, while the valleys between the great rivers and around the mountainous regions provide rich pasture land, similar to that found in the rich steppe districts of the central part of eastern Europe.

There are then, in this Europe which we are presently considering, twenty-two countries owning to one hundred and twenty-one different breeds or types of ponies and horses. The same breed may appear in several other countries; for example, the *Lipizzaner* is an Austro-Yugoslav breed, which is also bred in Hungary, but is famous because of its connection with the Spanish Riding School in Vienna.

The breeds of ponies and heavy horses are not so numerous as are the warm-blood strains, which have been built up from one or both these breeds crossed with a hot-blood (*Thoroughbred* or Oriental).

POLAND

The ponies of Europe are of extremely ancient origin. The *Tarpan*, now to be found in the Bialowieza Forest, Poland, used to roam in vast herds, but by the late middle ages was becoming rare. His descendants—the *Konik*, the *Huzul*, the *Bosnian*, the *Gotland* and the now extinct *Lofoten* pony—share many characteristics, which include the predominant dun, mouse-dun and blue-dun colour. The *Huzul* has acquired a considerable amount of Arab blood and this has 'nicked' in a most satisfactory manner. especially in the local Carpathian breed. The *Huzul* has recently been introduced to the south of England.

As a country Poland has been famous for centuries for her tradition of horsemanship. In 1955 there were around three million horses in the country. These are used to a large extent in agriculture and it is not unusual to meet an eight-in-hand team of light horses pulling a threshing machine! There are forty-two main studs with anything from fifty to over two hundred stallions of different breeds standing at some of them.

The main object at the present day is to breed a well-bred light horse up to weight. The *Masuren* horses meet this demand. The breed is based almost entirely on the old *East Prussian* blood lines, as is the *Poznan* horse. *Oldenburg, East Friesian, Furioso, Gidran* and of course *Arabs* are also used.

The *Sokólsk* breed of horses, generally little known in Western Europe, is found in the Grodny district of the Byelorussian republic of the U.S.S.R., in the Novograd district (Ukraine), in Wilno (Lithuania) and in the Bialystock district of Poland. A very similar breed is the *Ermland* or *Stuhm,* found in West Prussia and the Mazurian Lake district. The *Sokólsk* originated about a hundred years ago. (See pp. 39-46).

GERMANY

Germany has two native pony breeds—the *Dülmen,* which lives in a semi-wild state in the Meerfelder Bruch, and the hardy almost extinct *Senner* pony in the Teutoburger Wald, to the south of Osnabrück. In Westphalia the *Hanoverian* horses have their origin in these two local native breeds.

Germany once had the largest number of specified warm-blood breeds of horses in western Europe and the most valuable of them all was the *Trakehner* or *East Prussian.* This breed originated from the *Panje* (Pan = master) and the *Schweiken,* or local pony, similar to and descended from the *Konik,* which was to be found from Silesia in the south to the Baltic States in the north.

The stud at Trakehnen in East Prussia was founded in 1732 with a collection of stallions belonging to a number of different breeds, although the greater percentage were *East Prussian.*

The *Thoroughbred* stallion Perfectionist (by Persimmon–Perfect Dream) was imported from England to Trakehnen as a four-year old and although he was at stud for only three years (he suffered a fatal accident in his box) he sired a hundred and thirty-one foals. Of these thirty-two were stallions and thirty-seven were brood mares, and his blood appears in all the pedigrees of present day *East Prussian, Trakehner, Masuren* and *Russian Trakehner* horses*. Between the two World Wars 32,000 horses were exported annually from East Prussia.

* *Die Pferde mit der Elschschaufel* (Author).

23

As Soviet troops entered East Prussia in January and February, 1945, the inhabitants had to leave hurriedly. They harnessed their in-foal mares to their wooden field wagons and, under the most appalling conditions and difficulties, these incredibly courageous animals brought their owners to safety in the west, after a trek of nine hundred miles. Most of the foals were born dead through starvation. Fewer than a thousand pure-bred *Trakehner* and *East Prussian* horses escaped (see *Masuren,* p. 43) and they covered the distance unshod and with very little to eat, in snow, frost and under bombing in about two and a half months. During this time most of them stood outside during the night and were never unharnessed. This is the greatest endurance test that horses of any breed have ever been asked to undertake. About thirty-three stallions in the care of an old groom and two boys were driven to the west. With this nucleus in western Germany, breeding of *Trakehner* horses, which is a fixed breed, is continued.

It has become a lighter, more elegant saddle horse—but still with plenty of bone—than its cousin, the *Masuren.* Studs are at Schmoel, Rantzau and Planker in Schleswig-Holstein and at Zweibrücken in the Pfalz. The main stud in the Solling, Western Germany, breeds stallions for use in other warm-blood breeds, particularly for the *Hanoverian,* Land Hanover, which has now become the most important breed of light horses in West Germany.

Formerly a carriage horse *par excellence,* especially during the reign of George II, who was also Elector of Hanover, the *Hanoverian* is now proving of great value as a saddle horse for practically all competitive events. The rather straight shoulder of the harness horse has been improved, combined with a well-set neck and good wither; the convex head, inherited from the *Neapolitan* of the 15-16th century, has now almost entirely disappeared in favour of the well-bred head of the *Trakehner* or *Thoroughbred.*

At Celle there is one of the biggest state-owned studs, where about two hundred *Hanoverian* stallions stand between seasons. These sires are used to cover about 8,500 mares owned by farmers throughout the Province. As with most European breeds of warm-blood stallions, a riding, driving and endurance test is required of them as three-year-olds before they are granted a licence.

For the past fifty years the stallions give exhibitions lasting nearly three hours at their Stallion Parade held in the autumn. They are driven in sulkies, ridden to music, jumped, driven in teams of ten-in-hand by liveried coachmen, in the royal coaches, and in Roman quadrigas. Three unbridled stallions give a free dressage display, obeying a riding master who stands in the centre of a small arena.

There are several studs for *Trakehner* horses in other countries—U.S.S.R., Bulgaria, Rumania, Spain, Canada, Brazil, Colombia, East Africa, India. Quite recently a few brood mares and a stallion have been exported to England, where there is also a small *Hanoverian* stud.

Other West German warm-blood breeds are the *Oldenburg* of northern Germany and the *Holstein*. The *Oldenburg* was originally based on the local *Friesian-Oldenburg*, but later *Cleveland Bay* blood was introduced and still later *Norman*, resulting in a heavier all-purpose horse—although some lines have *Thoroughbred*–Dark Ronald blood. The *Holstein* has lately ceased to have a stud of its own, but is still bred by farmers in the Emshorn district of Holstein. The *Thoroughbred* stallion, Cottage Son, was imported eight years ago and is producing some first class stallions. (See pp. 47-57).

East Germany, which is at present rather cut off, breeds extensively the *Oldenburg-East Friesian* in Thuringia. The *Mecklenburg* breed is up against some difficulties as there is no main stud, but within recent years two *Anglo-Arab* stallions have been used successfully and the breed is basically the same as the *Hanoverian*. Brandenburg has a lighter soil with a maritime-continental climate and consequently a lighter horse can be used. The breed, having almost disappeared, was established again after 1945; the main stud is at Neustadt an der Dosse. From a minimum of two stallions, there are now a hundred and sixty stallions representing the breed.

HUNGARY

Horses are increasing in this country and some most beautiful animals are bred here (see *Arabs*, p. 60). The Mezöhegyes stud, south-east of Budapest, was founded in 1785 and *Large Nonius, Small Nonius, Furioso-North Stars* and *Shagya Arabs* are bred. The *Large Nonius* is a hard, middle-weight suitable for riding, driving or farm-work. It is based on *Anglo-Norman* blood through the *Anglo-Norman* stallion Nonius, born in 1810, who was captured in 1815 from the French Stud Rosières (Zweibrücken). The *Small Nonius* possesses more *Arab* blood than the *Large Nonius*, is finer and shorter on the leg, and has considerable stamina. Both Furioso, bought in 1841, and North Star (1844), who were *Thoroughbred* and *Norfolk Roadster* stallions, founded a first-class breed of warm-blood horses suitable for all purposes. A private *Furioso* stud is situated in Bavaria. *Nonius* and *Gidran* studs are also to be found in Bulgaria, which also has its own native mountain pony generally used as a pack pony. (See pp. 58-60).

SPAIN AND PORTUGAL

An extraordinary similarity in conformation and colour is found between the *Sorraia* pony of Spain and the *Tarpan (Equus przevalskii gmelini* Ant.) of Poland (see p. 39). The west of Spain and Portugal is the homeland of this breed and of another, rather larger, the *Garrano* or *Minho* ponies. It is exciting to find that the *Garrano* pony (possibly descended from *E. przvalskii*), which forms about three-quarters of Portugal's equine population, was the model many thousands of years ago for Paleolithic man's cave paintings. Comparison also shows that the *Connemara* pony of the old Rosemuck strain and the Western Islands pony of Scotland have many similar points to the *Sorraia*—dun, with darker points, dorsal stripe, sometimes wither stripes and very often zebra marks on the fore and hind legs.

The *Andalusian* breed of horses dates back to the Moorish invasions, when *Barbs* or *Berbers,* as they are sometimes called, and *Arabs* were crossed with the local Spanish horses and ponies; for undoubtedly the *Sorraia* and the *Garrano* contributed to the origin of the *Andalusian,* just as they have done to the *Criollo* of South America (pp. 256-260). In turn the *Andalusian,* which is bred near Cordoba and Seville, and probably to a lesser extent the *Lusitano* and *Altér* of Portugal, considerably influenced —and, in fact, helped to found—a number of other breeds which gained considerable importance in the Middle Ages: the *Neapolitan* of Italy, the old *Norman,* the *Friesian (Harddraver),* the *Frederiksborg,* the *Hackney,* several of the German warm-blood breeds, the *Kladruber* and especially the *Lipizzaner.* (See pp. 61-64).

CZECHOSLOVAKIA AND AUSTRIA

During the late Middle Ages both the *Lipizzaner* and the *Kladruber* were parade horses of the first importance. Spotted and coloured horses were regarded with especial favour as anybody can see when studying old prints of the period. The *Kladruber* of Czechoslovakia was a classical coach horse as well, and the old blacks belonging to the royal mews in Vienna performed their last duty in 1916 when drawing the funeral carriage of the Emperor Franz Joseph, the man who had reigned since 1848.

The Spanish horse had an important rôle in founding the *Lipizzaners* of the Spanish Riding School, Vienna. Their pedigree is a guide to their Spanish ancestry—Conversano, Neapolitano. *Kladruber* blood is also found in the Favoury and Maestoso lines; while the Pluto line brought *Frederiksborg* blood; Siglavy *Arabian* and an especial line came from Incitato of the Fogaras Stud in Transylvania.

These horses are world-famous for their splendid High School displays given every Sunday during the summer months. It takes seven years to train a horse, who can be expected to attain perfection only in one or two movements at which he then specialises, and it takes twelve years for a rider to become a fully qualified 'Bereiter'.

The stud is at Piber. All subsequently grey horses are born black, although there are bay and brown *Lipizzaner* horses. They mature late, but reach a ripe old age and some are still capable of performing complicated High School movements at twenty-five years old. Only the famous greys are used in quadrilles. In Austria and Hungary both *Lipizzaner* and *Kladruber* horses are used for harness work and in agriculture.

Wherever a small, strong, hardy pack-pony is needed there will always be a use for the chestnut *Haflinger.* The pony is much in demand in South Germany and Austria. The original home of this breed is South Tirol. An original *Arabian,* El Bedavi, was bred with an original *Arabian* mare, Koheil, in Bâbolna, Hungary, and produced El Bedavi II, whose descendants founded the present breed. The *Haflinger* pony has been described as a 'prince in front, a peasant behind'. (See pp. 65-68).

ITALY

In North Italy, the *Avelignese* is bred on the lines of the old *Abellinium–Haflinger* breed. It is said that in the mountainous regions of South Tirol a small pack-pony has been in use since prehistoric times. Indeed, an authority named Antonius was of the opinion that this pony was the descendant of an ancient European prehistoric breed of small ponies, which were subsequently crossed with the larger *Noriker,* which they closely resemble.

The Italian school of riding, which has long been world famous, has its headquarters at the Cavalry School of Pinerolo (Piedmont) and Tor di Quinto (Rome). Here the *Salerno, Maremine* and *Calabrese* breeds of horses are schooled for show jumping and other equestrian sports. *Thoroughbred* blood is used with good effect in these breeds. The Italian Trotting world is the greatest in Europe and the Italians are far more ardent fans of the *Trotter* than of the *Thoroughbred!* Their greatest *Trotter* is the chestnut stallion Tornese and the most important breeder in Italy is Count Orsi-Mangelli in Persicuto. On the islands of Sicily and Sardinia there are small mountain pony breeds much influenced by *Arab* and *Barb* blood. (See pp. 69-70).

FRANCE

The *Thoroughbred* and the *Anglo-Arab* are two of France's most highly valued breeds, which are recognised throughout the world.

The French 'races de demi-sang' are not as numerous as they were and are now represented by the *Anglo-Norman* or *Norman* of two types—saddle and cob. The latter is a good all-round animal. Normandy is an extremely old breeding district, and was known as such even before the days of William the Conqueror.

To Young Rattler (born 1811), an English half-bred stallion, fell the honour of establishing the *Anglo-Norman* breed. In sixteen years he got 376 foals. The breed became a useful carriage and saddle horse of excellent conformation and action and for many years provided a source of income to the province.

Today in the departments of Calvados and Manche are bred high-class riding horses, which may be seen competing at most international horse shows. *Norman* stallions have been used to improve other warm-blood breeds, such as the *Charollais,* the *Vendéen,* the *Charantais* and the *Breton,* and also in Switzerland, Germany and Belgium.

The *Camargue* ponies in the south of France live in a practically wild state upon the

27

marshy lands surrounding the mouth of the Rhône. Little is known of their history, but they obviously have a considerable amount of Oriental blood or else, as some hippologists believe, they are the descendants of a prehistoric race of horses, which would make them a very ancient breed indeed. By some they are thought to be the direct descendants of the Diluvial horse, whose bones have been found at Solutré in France. They are used as cow-ponies for herding the black Camargue bulls, and suffer much ill-usage in summer from the tourist trade and in winter from lack of warmth and food. The *Ariège* pony belongs to the Pyrenees; it is small, very energetic and hardy. (See pp. 71-75).

SWITZERLAND

Since the war Switzerland has been very busy building up her breeds of light horses, and there are fourteen new studs containing seven hundred mares. The horses which are being bred are saddle and working horses. The stud at Avenches breeds the heavier *Freiberger*—of *Norman, Breton, Percheron* and *Holstein* origin, but mated with Bâbolna *Shagya Arabs*. The warm-blood *Einsiedler* (stud also at Cloister Einsiedel) is fast becoming a notable cavalry and show horse.

To stress the ability of a fixed blood line to appear many generations later, attention should be paid to the photograph of the stallion Scipion (p. 76). Here is an almost perfect example of the once much-valued *Norfolk Roadster* of nearly two hundred years ago! The *Shagya Arab*, mated to a *Freiberger* mare, has produced in Scipion almost exactly the same result as the Darley Arabian did when crossed with local English mares two hundred and fifty years ago. The *Freiberger* horse should prove very good indeed. (See pp. 76-79).

THE NETHERLANDS

We come to the Netherlands with two excellent but little known breeds of horses—the *Gelderland* and the *Friesian*. The third, the *Groningen*, is fast dying out. The *Gelderland* breed of horses is again based on early *Spanish, Norman* and *Norfolk* blood. It has fine knee action, is active and energetic, and is used for light farm work, as a superb harness horse and for show-jumping. The *Friesian* is of Spanish descent, as the *Andalusian* was crossed with the ancient Friesland breed. In 1879 it was closely related to the *Groningen*, but by 1913 the breed was reduced to three stallions. Then a number of Friesian farmers got together and by very careful management re-established the old breed. It is regarded chiefly as a working horse, but is used both in harness and under the saddle. The *Friesian (Harddraver)* helped to establish the world's *Trotters*. Belgium has the *Belgian Warm-Blood*. (See pp. 80-83).

28

DENMARK

At one time Denmark was the foremost European country in breeding horses, with its Royal Frederiksborg stud, founded in 1562 on *Neapolitan* and *Andalusian* blood. The *Frederiksborg* horse was related to the *Lipizzaner* and was regarded by the cavaliers of the late Middle Ages as the best school and parade horse obtainable. Since the breed was practically 'sold out' and subsequently very inbred, nothing much remained, although the present lighter *Frederiksborg* has some of the old blood in his veins. The latter was very much crossed with the *Holstein*. A lighter animal bred upon the same lines as the *Frederiksborg* is the *Knabstrup ;* when spotted it is very popular for circus work. (See pp. 87-88).

SWEDEN

This country possesses a native pony breed in the hardy *Gotland* or *'Skogruss'*, bred on the island of Gotland in a more or less wild state. They are thought to be the immediate descendants of prehistoric horses. The stallion which has had a great influence on the breed was the *Gotland-Syrian* Olle, which brought the yellow dun colour into the breed. The *Oriental* stallion Khedivan introduced the grey colour.

The *Swedish* warm-blood horse has become a recognised breed. It is based on *Anglo-Norman*, *Arab* and *Thoroughbred* lines with a later introduction of *East Prussian* and *Hanoverian* blood. A definite type has been reached by the most careful selection at the Flyinge state stud. Introduction of foreign stallions has sharply declined during the past twenty years. 'Conformation and ability to jump are among the qualities most valued in stallions selected for stud purposes. For the past four Olympic Games, the Swedish Olympic Games team has been mounted entirely on home-bred horses with a large percentage of *East Prussian* blood'.* (See pp. 89-90).

NORWAY

Here there are three breeds of ponies—the little known *Northlands* (not unlike the *Iceland* pony or the *Welsh Mountain* pony) and the far more widely known and used *Fjord*, *Norwegian* or *Westland* pony as the breed is variously called, with its characteristic dun coat—in several shades—dorsal stripe and upright silver and black mane, which is clipped to keep its position. The *Fjord* breed is fairly old and has not changed much since the Viking period; it may be regarded as indigenous to Norway, although a number of other countries have found an economical use for ponies of this breed in agriculture on light soil.

The *Fjord* pony is very tough, willing and good-tempered. The conformation may not always be correct, but the ponies seldom suffer any of the ordinary equine illnesses.

---

* *Handbuch der Tierzüchtung: Rassen Kunde.*

29

Farmers on the lighter soils of Germany have adopted these ponies in a big way, and Denmark has used the *Fjord* increasingly since the beginning of the century.

Much the same may be said of *Döle-Gudbrandsdal* pony, which is somewhat larger and really almost a cold-blood horse. The breed is fairly recent having been founded during the 19th century from native ponies, heavy Danish stallions, *Thoroughbred* and *Trotter* stallions. The *Döle Trotter* is a good harness pony (not really a pony perhaps) very active, hardy and good-natured, and may be put into the same class as the *Finnish* horse (p. 150). (See pp. 91-94).

GREECE

In the past Greece had several breeds of horses or ponies. They were usually fairly small; today there are very few left and the country cannot be termed traditionally equestrian.

The poet Oppian (c. 211 A.D.), in his poem on hunting, mentioned three breeds of pony—*Achean* (Peloponnese), *Thessalian* and *Thracian*. Xenophon (430-356 B.C.) tells us that the *Thessalian* was the most noted for beauty, courage and endurance. Equally valued were the *Argive, Acarnanian, Arcadian* and *Epidaurian* breeds. At the present day, Peneia, in the Peloponnese, has a local breed of pony used for farm work; also used by farmers in the mountainous regions of Thessaly and Epirus are the *Pindos* ponies. The small ponies from the island of Skyros, in the Aegean, are very similar to the *Tarpan* group (see p. 39). These ponies are often used on the mainland to teach children to ride.

The Cyclades islands also have a breed of tiny pony, and small ponies are sometimes to be found on the mainland, without being identified with a particular breed. In Thessaly, a light horse of Oriental stamp is used. (See pp. 95-96).

UNION OF SOVIET SOCIALIST REPUBLICS

The U.S.S.R. has by far the greatest number of warm-blood breeds of horses in Europe, and possibly the world, but this is scarcely surprising when it is realised that the Union consists of fifteen republics, made up of individual countries with their varied climates, cultures and, obviously, breeds of horses. In 1913 there were 35 million horses, in 1950 there were said to be 13·7 million, consisting of mountain horses, forest horses, steppe horses and imported breeds. And although rightfully some belong to the Asiatic group, for convenience they are included here within the term Europe.

The Baltic states of Esthonia, Latvia and Lithuania have several native breeds founded upon the *Konik*, with the *Viatka, Pechora* and the better-known and very ancient *Zemaituka,* which takes its name from the western Lithuania. These breeds, like almost all the primitive breeds of horses, possess an almost unbelievable stamina and capacity for endurance. Their legs are of iron and, like the *East Prussian* horses in their trek in 1945, they have been known to work and live for weeks on nothing more than the thatch from ruined houses. The *Zemaituka* has indeed almost made an art of hunger! The original breed has been much spoilt by cross-breeding and exportations. The *Viatka* pony, usually dun, palomino or chestnut with dorsal stripe, is bred to two types: *Obwinski* and *Kasanski,* in the Kasan province.*

The *Klepper* is founded upon *Arab* and *Ardennes* blood. *Klepper* stallions have been used to improve the *Obwa* or *Obwinski* ponies—used principally for transport and bred on the banks of the river Obwa—and those in the Kasan province.

The *Don* horse belongs to the steppes, and is one of the better-known warm-blood breeds; it is the ideal cavalry horse and was the mount of those crack cavalry men, the Cossacks. These horses have been bred up from the original *Mongolian-Kalmuck* crossed with Oriental, *Turkmene, Thoroughbred, Anglo-Arab, Persian* and most particularly *Karabair* (p. 107). *Orlov-Rostopschin* blood was also used to improve on the *Old Don* horse.

Like all the Russian steppe breeds, the *Don* horses are herded to graze on the steppes and are quite unaccustomed to paddocks as are other European breeds. Endurance tests under the saddle are: 283·5 km. (170 miles), in 24 hours, the last 4,600 metres at the trot.

The *Tscherkesser* horse is also closely related to the *Don*; it can adapt itself to cold and rain and is a safe mount on dangerous mountain passes. The *Kabardin* is considered the best of all mountain riding horses, and when crossed with the *Thoroughbred* is known as *Anglo-Kabardin* and is used to improve other breeds.

Near Tiflis, capital of the Georgian republic, we find the *Karabair* in three types. It is an old local breed used in harness, for pack transport and under the saddle. Their endurance test is 75 km. (45 miles) in 3 hours, 32 minutes over hilly country.

Of all the Russian breeds of horses the *Achal-Teké* is probably the most interesting and readers should compare the photograph on page 110 with that of the Persian Arab on page 185. If we are looking for an ancestor to the *Arab* and also to other Oriental breeds, we might well find it in the *Achal-Teké* and through him, the *Turkmene*. These are genuine desert horses. They run in herds—a 'Tabun' of 10-12 mares to one stallion, under the control of a herdsman. Their gait is that of a pacer and they are therefore most comfortable rides. Endurance test 4,300 km. (1,780 miles), of which six hundred miles were covered over a pathless, waterless, sandy desert. Like every other Russian breed the *Achal-Teké* has proved himself as a representative of the breed.

The one questionable thing about these Russian endurance tests, by the way, is: are the individual horses any good afterwards, or did the test have a bad effect on them? This question applies to a certain degree to endurance tests (even Olympic

* *Handbuch der Tierzüchtung: Rassen Kunde.*

31

Horse Trials) of any nature. Horses in general have a tremendous amount of courage and a great willingness to do their utmost. At the same time some people regard them as an expendable unit and, having very little knowledge of the physical fitness required of *every* horse undergoing any kind of endurance test, apparently overlook the possibilities of a 'broken heart'.

Through the Oriental breeds which have been brought to the British Isles over the centuries it seems therefore very likely that *Thoroughbreds* have *Turkmene* blood in their veins. (See pp. 98-114).

BRITISH ISLES

England has five native pony breeds: the *Exmoor, Dartmoor, New Forest, Fell* and *Dales.* Wales has its famous *Welsh Mountain* pony from whom have sprung three types: the *Welsh* pony, the harness pony and the cob. Scotland has two breeds now registered as one—the Western Isles merged into the Mainland *Highland* pony— and the indomitable *Shetland* pony. Ireland has her *Connemara* pony improved by the infusion of Spanish *Barb* and *Arab* blood from the beginning of written history.

Recent inquiries failed to elicit any information regarding the *Irish Draught* horse which was already becoming scarce in 1917. The type was probably descended from war horses brought to Ireland—and possibly from other importations. The first entry in the stud book is Comet 1892, by Comet dam by Vanderhum or, as in other entries, 'dam's breeding unknown'. Pictures of early *Irish Draught* horses show an uncommon likeness to several other European warm-blood breeds and very possibly breeding was on similar lines.

The *Irish Hunter* is well-known and is usually a brilliant jumper; many other countries buy these horses for competition in International show-jumping classes.

The history of Britain's native ponies is the history of Britain herself—for the one has been dependent upon the other. The oldest of them all, the *Exmoor* pony, has quite probably been in these islands for some thousands of years. The colour is dun or brown with the characteristic mealy nose and 'toad' eye. Similar colours are found in some *Fell* ponies, whose native district is Westmorland and Cumberland. The *Welsh Mountain* pony is well-known, because this pony and those of the other sections in the stud book have been exported to many countries. The *Highland, Fell* and *Dales* pony are capable of carrying great weights—who has not seen a print or painting of a *Highland* pony with a stag across his back? Quite a number of other countries have imported *New Forest, Shetland* and *Exmoor* ponies and have now introduced their own stud books for these breeds.

These native ponies have given rise to other breeds which in turn have died out, after passing on their qualities to yet other breeds. For example, there is the *Norfolk Trotter* or *Roadster,* whose blood is in most of the trotting horses of the world and in

A HERD OF TARPAN. The Tarpan (*Equus przevalskii gmelini* Antonius) is one of the most interesting breeds in Europe. In its wild state it was once very numerous and its territory extended from the Caucasus throughout Western Europe. (*Photographed on the Sperding Lake, Masuria (East Prussia), by the author*)

33

AN EAST PRUSSIAN STALLION. Hudamas carries the brand of double elk antlers and was photographed at the State Stud, Posadowo, Poland. This is a wonderful country for horse-breeding, where light horses are still in general use on all the farms and also in wagons and carriages of all sorts. (*Photograph by the author*)

some other warm-blood breeds. There is also the extinct *Galloway* of the north, which was used for racing, before Charles II made an institution of it at Newmarket, and which doubtless helped to give British mares the stamina to lay the foundations for the British *Thoroughbred*. This wonder of scientific horse-breeding has become an industry on practically the same site that Queen Boadicea, or Boudicca, occupied for breeding *her* 'Celtic' ponies.

There have been many books written on the *Thoroughbred* horse. The term refers to a special breed of horses whose origins go back to the beginning of the 18th century. These horses filled the need then, as every breed of horses in every generation has filled some need, for the Englishman's love of sport combined with risk. Racing was not unknown in England prior to this period; at first races were confined to two adversaries who 'made a match' one against the other, and fortunes were won or lost.

The entire *Thoroughbred* breed is descended from three stallions—the Darley Arabian, the Godolphin Arabian and the Byerley Turk—and about forty original foundation mares, many of whom were 'plaine bredde' mares possessing quite possibly a fair amount of Oriental blood mixed with good plain native stock. Until 1770 Oriental stallions were used almost exclusively, but from then on home-bred stallions became more and more popular. The General Stud Book (G.S.B.) was founded by James Weatherby in 1791.

The early flat races were run in heats over courses of from two-five miles, so that the winner may have covered sixteen miles at racing speed in one day. As the horses also had to journey to meetings on their own feet, it is obvious that they had plenty of stamina, an attribute that today has to some extent given way to speed. Both fillies and colts are eligible to compete in the Derby, St. Leger and 2,000 Guineas, although usually the owners of fillies confine them to the 1,000 Guineas and the Oaks. These five are the 'Classic' flat races.

Steeplechases and hurdle races require horses with speed, stamina and jumping ability. The entries for these events are mares and geldings and sometimes stallions. One of the earliest steeplechases was run in Ireland in 1752 over $4\frac{1}{2}$ miles of open country; the first steeplechase over a course of 3 miles was run at Bedford in 1910. Although horses taking part in these races today are almost always *Thoroughbred*, like the point-to-point horses they may be part or three-quarter bred, which means that they may own to part hunter blood.

Point-to-points were originally run over open country round a church spire and back—or from church spire to church spire. Now most of the races are confined to fixed courses over a number of obstacles.

Great Britain may therefore be said to have provided the world with sprinters, stayers, hurdlers and steeplechasers. *Thoroughbred* stallions have been used to improve many other breeds; these stallions are used on native and part-bred mares to get good hunters. (See pp. 115-124).

Before the days of coaches, when merchandise such as wool, cloth, corn and pots were carried by pack on horses' backs, the travelling salesmen were called chapmen and so the horses they used became known as *Chapman* horses. They were good, strong horses. Later, when they were bred in the Cleveland district of Yorkshire and when coaches came into use during the reign of Elizabeth I, there was a demand for strong coach horses, which the *Cleveland Bay* fulfilled admirably. Farmers also used these horses in agriculture when oxen became too slow. Later, when coaches and carriages came into more general use on the improved roads—which formerly had consisted of rutted ways sometimes 300-400 yards wide—the 'Old Cleveland Bay' was improved by two *Thoroughbred* sires—Manica, by the Darley Arabian, and Jalap, by Regulus, by the Godolphin Arabian. The economy, longevity and lasting qualities of the breed were recognised all over the world.

Yorkshire Coach horses owed their origin to the *Cleveland Bay* and *Thoroughbred* and were magnificent animals. Both breeds were extensively exported; today there is a greater demand for *Cleveland Bays* than can be met. These horses stand about 16 hands high, and may often be seen in Yorkshire or, on state occasions, drawing the royal coaches in London. (See p. 125).

A number of *Spotted Horses* have been imported into Britain at various times and it may be less confusing to include them here. It is difficult to say in which country the *Spotted Horse* originated, but their colour is probably very ancient, since they are depicted on Chinese works of art and even earlier on the cave walls of Pêche-Merle, France.

In 1575 King Frederick II of Denmark founded the Royal Frederiksborg Stud, and later the initials of Christian VI were used as the brand of the Spotted Stud, still later known as the *Knabstrup* horses (see p. 88). These Spotted horses were immensely popular at European Courts in the 16th and 17th centuries.

A number of *Neapolitan* and *Spanish* horses were used in the foundation of the Frederiksborg Stud, which was closed in 1871, and it is probably due to the influence of the *Spanish* horse that the modern *Knabstrup* owes his colour.

A similar type of Spotted horses, called the *Appaloosa*, was also developed by the Nez Percé Indians of Central Idaho, in the United States. Another type of the same colouring is the *Colorado Ranger,* which claims descent from imported *Spanish* stock. Their coats are silky, sometimes white or partly red-roan with black or chocolate spots of different sizes; these can be felt with the fingers, as though they were superimposed. On the quarters the spots may be so close as to give occasionally the effect of a stripe; there is often much silver hair in the mane and tail. (See p. 242).

The *Hackney* horse and pony is another product of the British islands and is descended from the *Thoroughbred*, the *Norfolk Trotter* and the native pony. It is especially a showy horse with high action and plenty of courage and fire. In the old days they were expected to trot seventeen miles to the hour and to *complete* this distance within the hour! Because of their bone and powerful hocks several different

36

breeds of harness horses have been used to breed first-class show-jumpers and Event (Military) horses.

As entries in the Hackney Stud Book show, breeding began in 1755—and there are forty-three volumes of the Stud Book! Since the 1939-45 war the popularity of the *Hackney* has increased. These horses and ponies are still driven on the road and are used for private driving purposes—although they are more popular as a show ring spectacle and are a magnificent sight when driven tandem or pair! Yet they have not the quality of a few years ago. It has been said that when Black Magic of Nork died, the last great *Hackney* disappeared. Both *Hackney* horses and ponies have been exported to many countries including the United States, Canada, Spain, Italy, Australia, South Africa, Germany, Holland, Denmark and South America. (See pp. 126-127).

The Racing *Trotter* has a different action to the *Hackney,* although this breed shares the same ancestors, with a larger amount of *Harddraver* and *Thoroughbred* blood. The horses either trot—'tormentor'—with a long, extended, diagonal stride, or pace—'ambulator'—which is best described as a paralleled action similar to that of the camel, and otherwise known as the amble.

A number of European countries and the United States have their own particular breed of *Trotters.* Competitive trotting races were popular for many years in Russia. The *Orlov Trotter* breed was established in 1778 by Count Orlov Tschesmensky with the Oriental Smetanka, *Thoroughbred, Arab, Frederiksborg, Russian* and the Dutch *Harddraver.* The foundation sire was Bars 1, whose blood may be found in the pedigrees of most pure-bred *Trotters.* Bars 1 stood at the Czjenow stud for seventeen years. The horses were bred for racing in sulkies and sleighs. Count Rostopschin further improved the breed, partly by in-breeding, so that it is known today as the *Orlov-Rostopschin.*

The *Russian Trotter* breed was established towards the end of the last century by importing American horses and with them came new methods of training and breeding. Although no further horses were imported from the beginning of World War I, the new breed, though originally of *Orlov* strain, proved faster and harder than the latter. The horses are all used for transport and agriculture.

The Netherlands, Germany, Italy, France and the Scandinavian countries, the United States, Australia and New Zealand, where the sport is extremely popular, have their own trotting associations; the sport is also catching on in the north of Britain.

The Netherlands may be regarded as the cradle of racing *Trotters*—the Dutch *Harddraver*—since it was a national sport long before other countries took it up.

France has a special breed, the *Anglo-Norman Trotter,* or *Demi-Sang* (pp. 72-73), which are not only raced in sulkies but also under the saddle. Founders of the breed were the half-bred English stallion Young Rattler (possibly *Cleveland Bay),* the

Norfolk Phenomenon and the *Thoroughbred* The Heir of Linne. France now has over 6,000 registered *Trotters*. There are two new breeds of trotter derived from the older breeds—the crosses *Orlov* x *Standardbred*, now in Russia called Métis; and the French *Noram*, which springs from *Demi-Sang* x *Standardbred*. In addition there is one cold-blood trotter, the *North Swedish* (p. 148). Finland has a trotter bred up from the *Finnish Universal*, while Norway races the *Döle Trotter*.

There are studs in Europe for the following breeds of *Anglo-Arabs*:

GIDRAN: The Anglo-Arab of Hungary and south-east Europe.

SHAGYA ARAB: Hungary. The desert-bred Arabian stallion Shagya founded a breed from superior Oriental stock. Traditionally stallions are given the name Shagya and a Roman number, which shows to which generation the horse belongs.

STRETLETS ARAB: Russia. Ukraine native mares and *Anglo-Arab*, *Turkish*, *Persian* and pure *Arab*. Now breeds true with all the qualities of a big *Arab*.

HALF-BRED ARAB: Covers most continents.

ANGLO-ARAB: France. The French *Anglo-Arab* is the result of a long development, and the climate and soil of France have been ideal for the conservation of certain outstanding qualities. There were always large numbers of horses from the Pyrenees right up to the Charente; these were successively known as *Iberique, Navarrin, Bigourdan* and *Tarbais*.

Great losses were sustained by these breeds during the various wars and revolutions, but fresh *Arab* blood was brought in again during the Napoleonic campaigns. Breeding was reorganised in 1806 and the south Pyrenean region was supplied with stallions from Andalusia, as well as *Barbs* and *Arabs* from the Emperor's private stables. About sixty years later the Pompadour Stud imported English *Thoroughbreds* and thus the *Anglo-Arab* came into existence—and a first-class saddle horse was born.

The success of *Thoroughbred* blood was so great that it was abused and, in order to preserve the qualities of hardness and endurance required of the *Anglo-Arab*, certain restrictions had to be placed on the use of the *Thoroughbred*. Finally the mixture of *Thoroughbred* and *Arab* blood was stabilised in the production of the *Anglo-Arab* saddle horse, which must have at least twenty-five per cent *Arab* blood to be eligible for the stud book. The result is a delightful saddle-horse which combines the speed of the *Thoroughbred* with the stamina and handiness of the *Arab*. These qualities have put the breed at the top of many big International events.

Anglo-Arabs bred at Pruchna in Poland have also proved themselves to be a great asset in winning International events, and a number have been bought by various Olympic teams.

Locality: Poland–Popielno, Bialowieza, Haras Hubno, Grojec.

Colour and characteristics: Brown and mouse dun, with dorsal stripe, dark mane and tail, intermingled silver hairs, sometimes stripes on forelegs and inner thighs; coat may change to white in winter. Long head, slightly convex face, bulging at the nostrils; longish ears; short, thick neck, good shoulders; long back; sloping quarters; fine legs. Very fertile.

Height: About 13 h.h.

Tarpan (Equus Przevalskii Gmelini Ant.)

The *Tarpan (Equus przevalskii gmelini* Ant.) is a breed over which there rages heated argument. Up to 1870 there were a number of wild herds of steppe *Tarpan* in Eastern Europe, Bialowieza, the Caucasus and further into Russia. In 1879 the last wild *Tarpan* had been killed near Askania Nova and in 1887 the last animal in captivity died. At this time Polish authorities collected from the peasant farms a number of animals which bore all the necessary qualifications and put them into the Forest Reserves at Bialowieza and Popielno. The peasants had been in the habit of catching the steppe *Tarpan* when they required cheap ponies on their holdings. It is argued that these horses are not true *Tarpan,* but none the less they are remarkably alike in all respects: they are extremely fertile, and they may change their coats to white in winter, like other true feral animals when subjected to Arctic conditions.

Konik

Locality: Poland–East of the San river.

Colour and characteristics: Yellow, grey and blue dun. Well-proportioned,
often cow-hocked. Good tempered, willing, frugal, long-lived,
very fertile.

Height: About 13·1 h.h.

The nearest domesticated relative to the *Tarpan* is the *Konik,* which has rather better conformation than the local *Panje* ponies—small horses. These and the *Huzul,* which is very probably the mountain variety of the *Konik,* belong to the north-eastern European group. The *Konik* is found in widely spread areas east of the river San, and has laid the foundation for almost all breeds of Polish and Russian horses—at least those breeds found in western Russia. This *Konik* stallion, Kamien, is blue dun, with dorsal stripe.

40

Huzul

The *Huzul* is smaller than the *Konik,* a willing, fearless and tireless mountain pony, 'who makes an art of starvation'—in other words is an economical feeder. A great deal of *Arab* blood has been introduced, but in Galicia the breed is considered to be a fairly pure descendant of the *Tarpan.* The pony should have a short, high action. It is also known locally as the 'Carpathian pony'. The foal is only a few days old.

Locality: Poland–Carpathians.

Colour and characteristics: Prominent dun shades; also dark colours; rarely grey. Characteristic *Tarpan* head, good neck and sturdy, rather over-built body; short sloping quarters; inclined to be cow-hocked; joints occasionally wanting. Of great endurance, hardy and willing.

Height: 12·1 to 13·1 h.h.

Sokólsk

Locality: Poland and U.S.S.R.

Colour and characteristics: Generally chestnut. (A very similar breed, the *Ermland* or *Stuhm*, is chestnut, brown or grey). A working horse, easy tempered, economical and hard; almost clean-legged.

Height: Varies from 15·1 to 16·1 h.h.

The *Sokólsk* breed was founded about a hundred years ago and later improved by the chestnut Norfolk-Breton stallions, Upas Jarboter, imported from France in 1920, and Zizi and Marquis II; and also the pure Belgians, Miemic and Mumm, the Anglo-Norman, Vaudeville, and a number of Ardennes stallions. The horse seen here, near Brest–Litovsk, is harnessed in the Russian style to a long, wooden, rubber-tyred field wagon common throughout Eastern Europe.

42

Masuren

When the Germans evacuated Eastern Germany in the winter of 1945, many of their horses had to be left behind. At the end of the war the Poles took over most of the old studs and horse breeding began again. Among the breeds is the *East Prussian*, now called the *Masuren*. Some of the older animals bred in East Prussia bear the double elk antler brand, while the present-day young *Masuren* horses carry the brand of the particular stud where they were bred.

Locality: Poland
(East Prussia).

Colour and characteristics:
All colours with exception piebald and skewbald; many chestnuts and bays.
Well-made, well-proportioned saddle horse, also used for draught purposes. Willing and indomitable worker.

Height: About 16 h.h.

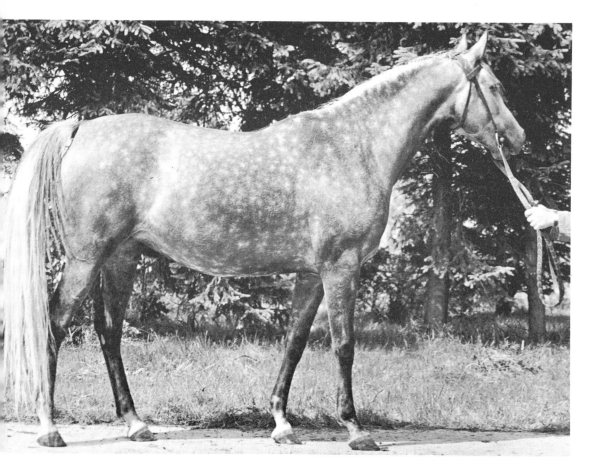

Polish Arab

Locality: Poland–Janow Podlaski, Nowy Dwor, Albigowa, Michalów.

Colour and characteristics: All shades of grey, including flea-bitten grey, chestnut and bay. *Kuhaylan* type–i.e., especially masculine. Characteristic convex Arabian head and face; large, dark eyes; good neck and shoulders; short back and to some extent sloping quarters, with tail carried lower than in the *Siglavy* (the *Munighi* has a longer back and barrel).

Height: 14·2 to 15 h.h.

For a very long time *Polish Arabs* and *Anglo-Arabs* have had a world-wide reputation, for the Poles have always been considerable horsemen. The first mention of *Arabs* in Poland was in 1570, and a number of studs were founded, one of the most important was that belonging to Count Potocki. After the Second World war three new studs were created—Albigowa, Michalow and Nowy Dwor. Special races are held for these *Arabs* so that the breed can maintain the high standard required of them. Of the *European-Arabs* three types were bred—*Shagya, Dahoman* and *Gidran*. This is the pure-bred *Polish Arab* mare, Mortissa. (See Egyptian *Arab*, p. 195).

44

Locality: Poland–Poznan
district. Posadowo, Raçot,
Gogolewo Studs.

Colour and characteristics:
Firm colours. Compact
type of horse, very often
low to the ground;
conformation depends
upon percentage of
Thoroughbred blood;
eyes inclined to be small.

Height: About 16 h.h.

Poznan

The *Poznan* breed gets its name from the province to the west of Warsaw. It is a
superior middle and heavy-weight warm-blood horse, bred up from local *Konik* or
Panje mares and *Masuren* horses. Its breeding, in fact, is very similar to that of
the *Masuren*. It is used for agricultural work where a good, strong middle-weight
is needed on the medium soil. Where *Thoroughbred* or, through the *Masuren,* jumping
blood appears in its pedigree, the *Poznan* horse makes an exceptionally useful all-
round riding horse.

POLAND

Polish Anglo-Arab

Locality: Poland – Janow Podlaski.

Colour and characteristics: Bay, brown, etc., with white markings. Elegant saddle horse, with neat head and intelligent eye; well-proportioned neck; shoulder and withers; quarters sufficient. Straight mover with ability to jump.

Height: About 16 h.h.

The beautiful *Polish Anglo-Arab* stallion above is Schagya-Jantar. Below is a five-in-hand of grey *Anglo-Arabs;* compare this picture with other teams on pp. 60 and 63. The Potocki family, who were famous for their breeding of *Arabs* and *Anglo-Arabs,* were formerly one of the largest landowners in Poland.

Dülmen

Locality: West Germany.

Colour and characteristics: Any colour, but often brown/black.
Mixed breed.

Height: About 12·3 h.h.

The *Dülmen* pony, which runs in a semi-wild state within the confines of the Meerfelder Bruch, in Westphalia, has been bred there, it is said, since 1316. They are privately owned by the Duke of Cröy, who rounds up and sells off unwanted ponies at a gathering once a year. Stallions are sometimes imported from Britain and Poland. Efforts have also been made to prevent the extinction of the almost unknown, but extraordinarily hard, *Senner* pony, in the Teutoburg Forest of Hanover.

47

Locality: Now in West Germany, formerly East Prussia.

Colour and characteristics: No odd colours. Well-made saddle horse; good shoulder and quarters; thoroughbred head, sometimes lop ears; beautiful action and generally a good jumper. Delightful disposition.

Height: 16 to 16·2 h.h.

Trakehner

Of all the breeds of warm-blood horses in Western Germany, the *Trakehner* or *East Prussian* is the most valuable and the most outstanding. At present bred in private studs, the breed is a refugee from the Province of East Prussia, although the Polish Ministry of Agriculture has taken over the former East Prussian studs and the horses are being bred there on the old lines. This grey mare, Kassette, was one of the few to reach Western Germany on foot, after three months travelling, in 1945. Stallions are now used in several of the other German warm-blood breeds. The *Trakehner* horses are capable of great endurance and are invaluable for all kinds of mounted sports, and in their native land are used in harness and in agriculture.

The *Trakehner* stallion,
Abglanz.

Herr Willi
Schultheriss on
Thyra.

A group of
Trakehner mares.

Locality: West Germany–Province of Hanover. Lower Saxony.

Colour and characteristics: No odd colours. Developing into a new type. Strong, well-made saddle-horse. Generally distinguished action, and often with considerable jumping ability.

Height: 16 to 17·1 h.h.

Hanoverian

The *Hanoverian* is rather heavier than the *Trakehner*, which is used with the *Thoroughbred* to make this breed more versatile to fit in with today's demand for good riding horses. Formerley ideal carriage horses, and put to all uses on the farms, the *Hanoverian* now makes a good show jumper, hunter and dressage horse. The breed is widely spread in West Germany and has influenced the *Braunschweig, Mecklenburg, Pommern, Brandenburg* and *Westphalen* breeds. The main stud, where there are over 200 stallions, is at Celle. Below is a ten-in-hand of stallions! On p. 53 is Adonta, a 24-year-old *Hanoverian* mare.

A HERD OF TRAKEHNER MARES. Before the Second World War the stud at Trakehnen, East Prussia, was world-famous, but when the Russians entered the country in 1945 only a few hundred horses escaped to the West. They are now increasing again and are used in Western Germany in a variety of ways, both for work and for sport. (*Photograph by the author*)

A HANOVERIAN POLICE HORSE. This is Edler, ridden by Gendarmerie-Wachtmeister Knoop. The Hanoverian breed is widely distributed in West Germany, with the main stud at Celle, where there are over two hundred stallions. (*Photograph by the author*)

Adonta, a 24-year-old *Hanoverian* mare, with her 20th foal, aged two months.

Oldenburg

Locality: West Germany–Provinces of Oldenburg and East Friesland.

Colour and characteristics: Usual colours brown, bay, black, occasionally white markings. These horses belong to the same breed, and are the heaviest of the German warm-blood breed. Large, well-made cavalry/harness horse. Rather plain head, well-muscled neck and shoulder; compact, muscular back; good girth and barrel; tail set and carried high; short, strong legs with plenty of bone; hocks well let down.

Height: 16·2 to 17·2 h.h.

The *Oldenburg* has much the same uses as the *Holstein*, but is even a little heavier, although back in the pedigree can be traced the racehorse Eclipse, *Anglo-Arabs* and several other *Thoroughbred* lines; quite recently Norman blood was used when the stallion Condor was imported. Condor is pure-bred, but possesses 70 per cent *Thoroughbred* blood. *Oldenburg-East Friesian* lines are to be found in many southern and eastern European countries.

The *Holstein* is one of the oldest warm-blood breeds. Breeding dates from 1300 with the Marsh horse, which was bred up as a 'Great Horse for War and Tourney'. Oriental and Spanish blood was introduced and much later *Cleveland Bay*. The breed is required to be a strong riding and harness horse, of good conformation, plenty of bone and a great stride. It is often a good show-jumper and is also a first-class all-round animal for farmers to use.

GERMANY

Holstein

Locality: West Germany. Mainly bred nowadays in the Emshorn district of Holstein.

Colour and characteristics: Usually brown, bay/brown or black. Strong, heavy saddle/working horse.

Height: Up to 16·2 h.h. $9\frac{1}{2}$ inches of bone.

German Arab

Locality: West Germany.

Colour and characteristics: The type must change under different climatic conditions, and in North European countries horses of the Arabian breed tend to become larger. For other particulars see *Arab: Egypt,* p. 195.

The *Arab* is descended from Oriental horses of extremely ancient breeding. It first became an inhabitant of Arabia some fifteen hundred years ago. It was soon accepted by the nomad Arabs almost as a member of his family; it was hand-fed and its pedigree jealously guarded. The Oriental horse, whether *Arab, Barb* or *Turk,* found its way, generally as a gift to ruling potentates, to many countries outside Asia. Most European countries are enthusiastic breeders of these beautiful horses. The trappings are costly and should be especially noted. This German *Arab* mare is called Koranah.

56

Württemberg

Locality: West Germany–Stud Marbach.

Colour and characteristics: Usual colours brown, bay, chestnut and black, with white markings. A first-class middle-weight horse, used in agriculture and under the saddle. Straight but squarish head; keen eyes; good neck set on excellent shoulders; deep in the girth; strong loins; much bone; feet good.

Height: About 16 h.h.

The *Württemberg* horse has been developed from many other breeds—breeds as far apart as *Caucasian*, *Suffolk* and *Arab*, and the *Württemberg* became a 'cob' type which made it none the less useful for all types of work in the locality. The Stud Book dates back to 1895. The main stud is at Marbach, Württemberg.

German Shetland

Locality: West Germany. (*See* British Isles).

Shetland ponies are bred in West Germany and in appearance are much like those bred in the British Isles. They are valued for their work on small holdings and in horticulture in several other European countries apart from Germany.

Nonius

Locality: South-East Hungary–
Mezöhegyes Stud.

Colour and characteristics: Black and
dark brown. Medium/heavy
warm-blood horse, used for harness and
saddle. Very hard, reliable and willing.
Impressive head; long well-set neck;
good shoulders and withers; strong
chest and quarters; very active,
long stride.

Height: *Large Nonius:* Over 15·3 h.h.
Small Nonius: Under 15·3 h.h.

The Hungarians are first
and foremost a nation of
horsemen; and with
putzas—wide open grassy
plains—Hungary is a country
for horses. The studs—
Hortobágy, Mezöhegyes,
Kisbêr and Bâbolna—have
international repute. Best
known of the breeds are
Anglo-Arabs, Lipizzaners,
and the *Nonius*—large
and small.

Furioso

Locality: Hungary–
Mezöhegyes Stud.

Colour and characteristics: Black or
dark brown. Well-made, correct and
elegant saddle horse; very hard
and robust.

Height: About 16 h.h.

The *Furioso* mares *(below)* were bred at the Sarvar Stud, Hungary, and at the end of the last war were brought to the private stud at Leutstetten, southern Germany, where H.R.H. Prince Ludwig of Bavaria continues to breed *Furioso* horses. The photograph shows the horses winning the Three-day Driving Marathon at Aachen with no sign of tiredness. The *Thoroughbred* and *Norfolk Roadster* stallions, Furioso 1836 and North Star 1844, were imported to Mezöhegyes, Hungary, and crossed with *Arab* or *Anglo-Norman* mares of the *Nonius* breed. Later the *Thoroughbreds,* Vibar, son of Buccaneer (winner of the Ascot Gold Cup 1892), Dante and Nagyvezér were used. The stallion, Furioso XLV *(above),* is considered to have been one of the best stallions of his breed, whose purpose is to produce well-bred, active saddle horses.

Lipizzaner

Locality: Hungary–Bâbolna, Kisbér, Gyongyos and Szilvasvarad. (*See* Austria).

This is a *Hungarian Lipizzaner* five-in-hand.

Locality: Hungary–Bâbolna stud.

Colour and characteristics: Predominantly grey. Small head, concave or straight face; large, kind eyes; open nostrils; firm jaw; fine, arched neck moulded into good shoulders; well-sprung ribs; good quarters and loins. A well-made, elegant horse of excellent conformation; tail carried high; fine, silky coat. Appearance is of alertness and interest; good doer with plenty of stamina.

Height: About 15 h.h. 7¼ inches of bone.

Shagya Arabian

On the left is a *Shagya Arabian* mare. On the right 'Black Pearl of Hungary', the black *Arabian* stallion, O'Bajan XIII, born in 1949. Black is the rarest colour among *Arab* horses. O'Bajan XIII is principal stallion at the Hungarian State Stud, Bâbolna, founded in 1789.

Bâbolna has always had close connections with the Arab studs in Poland. The present director of the stud informs us that since its foundation 14,000 foals have been born there.

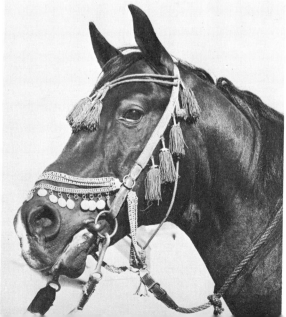

Locality: Western Spain and Portugal – River Sorraia and district.

Colour and characteristics: Generally dun, dorsal stripe and stripes on legs. Primitive breed with a long head, straight or convex face; long ears; thin ewe-neck, not very good shoulders, straight back and low-set tail. Conformation generally poor owing to poor grazing and climate; very tough and frugal, and able to withstand extremes of weather.

Height: About 13 h.h.

SPAIN

Sorraia (Garranos)

The *Sorraia* may be described as the native pony of Spain and Portugal, but it has not become as domesticated as the native ponies of other countries. It has remained true to the original type and a striking resemblance may be seen to both *Equus przevalskii przevalskii* Poljakoff and *Equus przevalskii gmelini* Ant. *(Tarpan)*. Although stripes on the legs are frequently present, together with the dorsal stripe, and the colour is not infrequently dun, their conformation follows more that of the *Tarpan,* as will be seen if pictures are compared (see p. 39). They are to be found on the poor campos lands just north of Lisbon, and along the river Sorraia into Spain. This is a typical *Sorraia* filly from the poorest pastures.

61

Andalusian

Locality: Spain–Seville district, Jerez de la Frontera.

Colour and characteristics: Grey, black or dark colours. Often convex or straight face; crested neck; full shoulders; sloping quarters; tail well-carried; strong legs, with short cannons and pasterns. Extremely elegant, proud horse with active, showy action; good jumper.

Height: Average 15·3½ h.h. but bigger horses are known–up to 16·3 h.h.

Weight: Average 1,280 lbs.

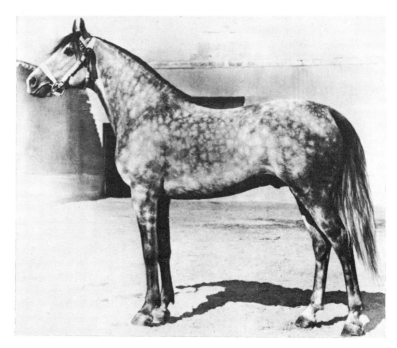

SPAIN

Apart from *Arabs* and *Carthusian* horses, Spain has for centuries been famous for the *Andalusian* breed of horses. When the Moors invaded Spain they brought with them Oriental horses, which, mated with Spanish horses, later became known as the *Andalusian*. The breed achieved wide renown as a parade horse during the middle ages and considerably influenced many breeds of horses in Europe during that time. Greys, palominos, duns and odd-coloured horses were fashionable. The *Andalusian* is distinguished by the roman nose and rather ordinary conformation—but his action is elegant and his whole manner of bearing himself one of great distinction. The horse below is showing the 'Paso de Andadura', a gait between the walk and trot.

A group of *Carthusian* mares and foals at the Terry stud (Puerto de Santa Maria, Cadiz).

Carthusian

Locality: Spain – Cordoba, Badajoz and Jerez de la Frontera State Studs.

Colour and characteristics: Generally grey. Slightly convex head on well-set neck; good conformation; Oriental type; intelligent and affectionate. Today many *Carthusian* horses are descended from the celebrated Esclavo.

Height: Average 15·3 h.h.

Spanish Arab

A *Spanish Arab* stallion and a five-in-hand.

Locality: Spain – Moratalla, Couil, Aracena, Olivenza and Almendralejo State Studs.

Colour and characteristics: Grey predominant, natural solid colours. Original *Arabians* (*see* Egypt).

Height: 14·2 to 14·3 h.h.

Lusitano

Locality: Southern and central Portugal.

Colour and characteristics: All solid colours. Fine small head; small ears and jaws; large eyes; well-placed if rather thick neck; exceptionally good shoulders and quarters; tail set lower than in some breeds; long forearm and thigh; full mane and wavy tail. Hard, frugal horse.

Height: 14·3 to 15·3 h.h.

Native to Portugal are two breeds of horses—the *Altér* and the *Lusitano*, and one pony breed, the *Minho*. Unfortunately, breeding of horses is sadly on the decrease. The *Lusitano* is very similar to the *Andalusian*, both being suitable for the saddle, harness or light farm work. This breed is found in central and southern Portugal. Its conformation shows quite a lot of daylight, or being 'up on the leg', with very good shoulders. The chestnut horse on the right was presented to H.M. Queen Elizabeth II by the President of Portugal.

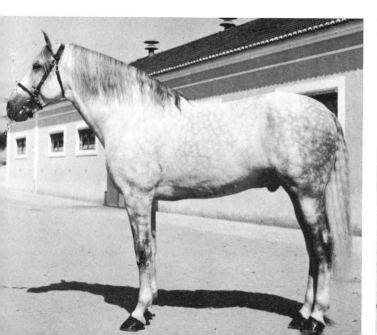

Kladruber

Locality: Czechoslovakia – Kladrub in Bohemia.

Colour and characteristics: Originally black or grey; at the present time, grey is general. Convex well-defined head; large, prominent eyes showing the whites; strong, erect, crested neck; long, straight back, with well-made, broad loins; good shoulders and quarters; tail set high and well carried; strong, clean legs and joints, hocks well let down; good hooves.

Height: 17 to 19 h.h.

The Spanish horse of the 16th and 17th centuries had a great influence on the sub-sequent *Kladruber* breed of horses, as well as on the *Lipizzaner*. The breed gets its name from the Stud Kladrub in Bohemia. Both breeds were in great demand by the Austrian Court as parade and coach horses, the *Kladruber* reaching a height of 17-18 hands. They were usually black or grey, but nowadays grey is most usually bred. The old breed almost died out at the end of the second world war, and a great deal of *Oldenburg, Hanoverian* and *Anglo-Norman* blood was then introduced.

65

Locality: Austria–Piber.

Colour and characteristics: Predominant colour is grey, sometimes bay, chestnut and roan. Foals born black. Big, sometimes convex head; large, expressive eyes; small ears; strong neck; compact body; strong rounded quarters; rather heavy shoulders; tail well set on and carried; short, strong legs, marked tendons and joints; small, hard hooves; thick, fine mane and tail. Willing, obedient, intelligent; very good character but matures late.

Height: 14·2 to 16 h.h.

Lipizzaner

The *Lipizzaner* is best known of all Austrian breeds, because of its connection with the famous Spanish Riding School in Vienna. It is a warm-blood horse with one of the oldest histories of such breeds. The region where these horses were originally bred was Karst, near Trieste, a district which the ancient Greeks also valued for horse-breeding. Indeed, the horses on the Parthenon Frieze in the British Museum remind one forcibly of the *Lipizzaner* executing a school movement.

Haflinger

Locality: Austria and Southern South Tirol, Germany; recently imported to Britain. In Italy, called *Avelignese*.

Colour and characteristics: Chestnut, almost always with full flaxen or lighter mane and tail; white markings allowed. Short-legged; strong quarters with broad back of the pack pony; hard joints and hooves. Large, lively eyes; big, open nostrils; small ears. Long, easy stride.

Height: About 14 h.h.

The *Haflinger* is bred in South Tirol, Bavaria and in many centres in Austria, to which country it belongs. It is the ideal mountain pony, because it can be used for all kinds of pack transport; even loads of hay are brought down the mountainside on its back. The *Haflinger* is a sure-footed riding pony and is often used in harness in carts and sleighs.

An elderly Austrian farmer with his fine *Haflinger*. (See previous page).

YUGOSLAVIA

Lipizzaner

Locality: Yugoslavia–Lipizzia, Kutjevo, Lipik, Fruska Gora, Purjavor, Dorbricevo. (*See* Austria).

The small farmers of Yugoslavia are very keen on the *Lipizzaner* horse for his constitution, stamina and activity. The breed is found, as it was in very early times, in the Karst region and in the north and north-west of the country. *Nonius* horses, *Arabs* and the extremely useful *Bosnian* pony, which now has a certain amount of *Arab* blood, are also bred in Yugoslavia.

Salerno

Locality: Italy – Maremma and Salerno.

Colour and characteristics: All colours. Well-made riding horse.

Height: About 16 h.h.

The *Salerno (Salernitano)* horse is bred in the Maremma, in Latium, north of Rome, and also in the Salerno valley. It is considered an excellent saddle-horse and is much in demand by the army. About 200 good brood mares are now kept. Traces of early Neapolitan blood may be found in some *Salerno* horses today.

69

Calabrese

Locality: Southern Italy.

Colour and characteristics: All colours. Warm-blood saddle horse.

Height: About 16 h.h.

Another breed, which again obtains its name from the district rather than to a distinct line of breeding, is the *Calabrese*, bred in Calabria, on the toe of Italy, as a riding horse. The Italian state organises all breeding, which is carried on in selected centres and studs.

Avelignese

The *Avelignese*, bred in the Trento area, and also in the hills of Venetia, Tuscany, Emilia and Central Southern Italy, has the same forebears as the *Haflinger* (see p. 67), being descended from the old *Avellinum-Haflinger*. The breed is said to have a considerable amount of oriental blood through the stallion, El Bedavi, who was bought by an Austrian commission in Arabia. The demand for the *Avelignese,* in view of its renowned qualities of fitness, docility and longevity, is increasing.

Locality: Northern and Central Italy.

Colour and characteristics: Chestnut, with light mane and tail; white markings. Short legged; strong, muscular quarters; hard joints and hooves. A draught/pack horse.

Height: About 14·2 h.h.

70

French Thoroughbred

Locality: France.

Colour and characteristics: All colours. (*See* Thoroughbred, under Great Britain). Special characteristic is that of the stayer, as opposed to sprinter, and these horses therefore represent the old type of English Thoroughbred. 75 per cent of races are over 2000 metres (1¼ miles). Two-year-old horses are not generally raced and French *Thoroughbreds* are therefore more developed.

Height: Varies according to breeding.

Representing the *Thoroughbreds* of France is Match III—on the left in the picture above. An outstanding winner on the flat at home, he won the King George VI and Queen Elizabeth Stakes at Ascot, and then went to America and won the Washington International. Match III now stands at stud in England.

Mandarin (above right), one of the greatest steeplechasers, has 19 victories to his credit, including the 1962 Cheltenham Gold Cup, the Hennessy Gold Cup (twice), the King George VI Chase (twice) and the Grand Steeplechase de Paris, where his equally famous jockey Fred Winter, O.B.E., steered him to victory with a broken bridle. Although bred in France, Mandarin did not distinguish himself until he raced in Britain.

FRANCE

Demi-Sang Trotter

Locality: France.

Colour and characteristics:
Any colour; white markings. Well-made saddle/harness horse (especially for trotting races). Good head and neck; marked wither; very strong back; tail sometimes a little low; good hard legs and well-defined hocks. A branch of the *Anglo-Norman* warm-blood breed.

Height: Average 16·2 h.h.

Like most other breeds of trotters, the *French Trotter* traces his ancestry back to the famous *Norfolk Trotter* of 130 years ago. It also possesses *Anglo-Norman* blood. The horse is rather bigger than the American trotter, and this is necessary because quite a large percentage of French races are under the saddle carrying weights of up to 85 kg. (11st. 6lb.) over long distances. Trotting races began in 1836, and it is estimated that there are now over 6,000 Trotters in France.

Noram Trotter

Locality: France (studs: Castillon-en-Auge, Calvados, and many other places); Italy (studs: Scuderia Kyra, Allevamento Groane, Allevamento Pontino, Gerardi Fulvio, etc.); and Austria (studs: Eggenberg, Kreuzenstein, Mariatrost, St Georg, etc.).

Colour and characteristics: Those of the trotter in general.

Height: Average 15·2 h.h.

Here are two of the world's leading *Noram Trotters*. On the left is the French-bred Hairos II. He was bought for Holland and now represents that country in international trotting races; he has won the World Championship in the United States. On the right is the Italian-bred chestnut stallion, Tornese, who won over £220,000 in eight years. During that time Tornese started 210 times and was first 129 times, second 58 times and third 13 times. He stands only 14 h.h.

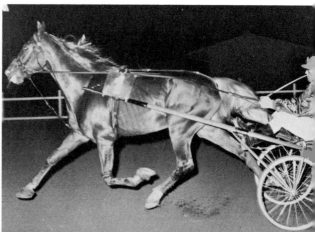

FRANCE

Norman

Locality: Two types.
France – Normandy;
in the Orne, Calvados and
La Manche districts.

Colour and characteristics:
Saddle horse: Any colour.
Compactly made; very
strong legs; short bone;
tail well carried. Best
type of military horse.
Height: Average 15·3 to
16 h.h.
Cob: Heavy cavalry horse.
Muscular, high, strong
withers; active, good
action; plenty of stamina.
Height: 15·3 to 16·1 h.h.

The *Norman* horse has developed two distinct types, both tracing their ancestry back to the *Norfolk Trotter*, Young Rattler, descended from the Godolphin Arabian. They have been carefully crossed and bred since the 17th century, reaching the height of their fame during last century as the best type of troop horse and carriage horse. The *Norman cob (below)* is also used in agriculture, while the saddle horse is being bred up into a most useful all-round riding horse, including the *Anglo-Norman Trotter*.

73

Camargue Pony

Locality: France – The Camargue region in the delta of the Rhône.

Colour and characteristics: Usually grey, flea-bitten grey, etc. Considerable hardiness.

Height: About 14·2 to 15 h.h.

The *Camargue* ponies live in a semi-wild state in the rather inhospitable, watery region around Arles, in the Rhône delta. When domesticated they are used as cow-ponies to guard the famous Camargue steers. Judging from their conformation they possess Oriental, probably Barb, blood. They have fine if long heads and often have goose-rumps, good shoulders and chests; owing to their rough pasturage, they are very hardy.

74

French Anglo-Arab

Locality: South-West France. Studs: Pompadour, Aurillac, Rodez, Villeneuve sur Lot, Pau, Tarbes.

Colour and characteristics: Any colour; white markings. Ideal saddle horse, with a good shoulder; deep in the chest; strong, hard legs; hocks well let down; long and supple action.

Height: About 16 h.h.

France has bred the ideal *Anglo-Arab.* It is a fine saddle horse, good-tempered and with plenty of stamina, has a good shoulder, with strong legs and bone, a good mover whose balance and natural ability make him an excellent jumper. It was originally based upon a number of Oriental breeds and, in order to restore losses caused by wars and revolutions, fresh *Arab* blood was introduced in 1806, and also stallions from Andalusia. The Pompadour Stud was founded about 1846 and a number of *Thoroughbred* stallions were imported from England, thus founding the breed of *Anglo-Arabs.*

75

Locality: Switzerland –
Avenches.

Colour and characteristics:
Blue roan, grey and other
hard colours with white
markings. A compact,
well-made, elegant horse,
standing square on all
four hard legs;
well-carried head and tail.
A horse of stamina;
steady, excellent character
and 'sound in wind
and limb'.

Height: About 15·3 h.h.

SWITZERLAND

Freiberger

In the stud at Avenches a light to
middleweight, well-made warm-blood
horse with good action and feet is being
bred today. The breed is based upon the
Freiberger type, having a certain amount
of the old *Freiberger* blood, *Norman*
and *Postier Breton* blood, and *Arab
Shagya* blood from the Bâbolna stud
in Hungary. The stallion, Scipion, shown
here as a foal and full grown, has
inherited conformation and weight from
his *Freiberger* dam, and his alertness,
kind disposition and stamina from his
sire, Shagya, 1940.

76

Einsiedler

Locality: Switzerland – Einsiedeln.
Colour and characteristics: Most hard colours. Colour and characteristics similar to the *Freiberger*. Used for military purposes.

Height: About 15·3 to 16·2 h.h.

Another ride-and-drive breed was the old *Einsiedler*—bred at Einsiedeln, south-east of Zürich—which has been revived on similar lines to the horses bred at Avenches. The Swiss army still use a number of warm-blood horses for all purposes, including this stallion, On y va.

77

Locality: Switzerland
(*See* France: *Norman*).

Swiss Anglo-Norman

Although prehistoric remains of various kinds have been found in Switzerland, the country had no native breed upon which to base subsequent breeding. Consequently horses have had to be imported both for riding and draught purposes.

The *Anglo-Norman* horse has proved extremely popular for remounts. As the demand for riding horses becomes greater breeding is increasing and between 6–700 mares are being used by fourteen warm-blood horse societies for this purpose.

Swiss
Holstein

Locality: Switzerland –
Wiental and East
Switzerland (*See*
Germany: Holstein).

A heavier horse is needed in the farming areas and the *Swiss Holstein* has proved a useful and hardy general purpose horse. The object is to get a good, well-grown ride and drive horse with a specially easy character.

Belgian Warm-Blood

Locality: Bred in many parts of Belgium, not a fixed breed.

Colour and characteristics: All colours; characteristics are those of a good saddle horse and/or trotter.

Height: Varies.

The *Belgian Warm-blood Horse* is considerably less known than the draught horse and is of comparatively modern development. There are two types—the riding horse and the racing trotter. Both types are evolved from breeds from other countries, and it is probable that France has helped in this.

80

Friesian

Locality: Holland–Friesland.

Colour and characteristics: Black without exception; very little white on face permissible. Strong, muscular, compact horse for harness and saddle; carries itself proudly, very active, high action at the trot. Profuse mane and tail and feather on its hard joints and legs; hard, open, blue hooves. Hard-working, loyal and sweet-tempered, but very sensitive, requiring intelligent handling.

Height: Average 15 h.h.

The *Friesian* comes of very old stock. It is a favourite subject in mediaeval paintings by the old Dutch Masters, as a knight's horse and, later, ridden by cavaliers. Although the breed faced extinction just before the first World War— in fact, the number of stallions was reduced to three—a committee was formed and by careful breeding and by crossing with the *Oldenburg,* the *Friesian* was kept alive. Today it is just as picturesque and as useful for all farm work as it was in the Middle Ages.

81

Two *Groningen* mares with their foals.

HOLLAND

Groningen

Locality: Holland–Groningen.

Colour and characteristics: Generally black or dark brown, with occasional white markings. Refined head and neck; strong back and deep body; clean legs. A docile, obedient working horse and heavyweight saddle horse.

Height: 15·2 to 16 h.h., although sometimes larger.

A typical lively *Gelderland* horse.

Gelderland

Locality: Holland –
Gelderland.

Colour and characteristics:
Chestnuts and greys
predominate; white on legs
and face is common. A good
sort of active saddle/harness
horse; makes a good jumper.
Rather plain head, medium
neck, good shoulders,
quarters and legs; tail is
carried exaggeratedly high.

Height: 15·2 to 16 h.h.

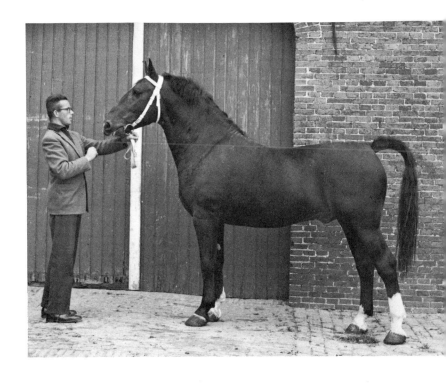

The *Gelderland* horse is lighter than his neighbour, the *Groningen*, which is fast dying out. The *Gelderland* traces his ancestry back to the Spanish and Neapolitan horse, and also has some *Norfolk Roadster* blood. It is a most active and showy harness horse, carries its tail very high after the prevailing fashion, and has proved itself a capable show-jumper.

Fjord

Locality: Denmark –
Especially Jutland (imported
from Norway).

Colour and characteristics:
Various shades of dun with
dorsal stripes, black points,
silver and black mane and
tail; mane is usually part
clipped. Strong sturdy pony
of good conformation; small
concave head, alert eye, very
active.

Height: About 14 h.h.

The *Norwegian* or *Fjord—Fjording*, as the breed is known in the Scandinavian countries—was imported into Denmark to help small-holders at the beginning of the century. From then until the present time about 16,000 have been imported. It makes an ideal harness pony, is extremely sturdy and is used for many types of farm work on lighter soil in Scandinavia and Western Germany. (See also p. 91).

A SPOTTED HORSE. Denmark has a breed of spotted horses called Knabstrup. Although imported from Denmark, this elegant spotted horse—Mr C. L. Carrick's Highway Rocket—was bred from an Arab sire and an Appaloosa dam and is not a Knabstrup. (*Photograph by John Nestle*)

THE QUEEN'S KARABAKH STALLION. Zaman, presented to H.M. Queen Elizabeth II by the government of the U.S.S.R., is a golden dun, pure-bred Karabakh stallion. These horses are bred for racing at the state stud in the Republic of Azerbaijan. Since his arrival in England, Zaman has been at stud. (*Photograph by John Nestle*)

Frederiks-
borg

Locality: Denmark –
Seeland and Bornholm.

Colour and characteristics:
Nearly always chestnut.
A medium light harness/
saddle horse, with light,
active action; good
conformation.

Height: Stallions about
16 h.h.; mares 15·2½ h.h.

Probably the best known and the oldest of the Danish breeds of horses is the *Frederiksborg*. The stud was first founded in 1562 with Spanish and Italian blood, and the horse was then used for school purposes. Since 1939, the breed having nearly disappeared, *Oldenburg* and *East Friesian* blood was introduced, so that today the horse is a very good type of driving horse, also capable of light farm work.

87

Knabstrup

Locality: Denmark.

Colour and characteristics: Very similar to the *Frederiksborg* and bred on the same lines. Its special characteristic is that it is a Spotted horse – e.g., with spots called blanket, leopard, raindrop, etc.

Height: About 15·3 h.h.

The *Knabstrup*, though similar to the *Frederiksborg*, is lighter and the breed is exclusively spotted. Breeding dates back to about 1808 when Spanish troops stationed in Denmark left behind a spotted mare called Flaebehoppen. The mare was of great speed and endurance and became the foundation dam. In recent times, bad crossing in order to obtain 'spots' has deteriorated the breed, and many so-called *Knabstrup* have very little relationship with the original breed.

88

Gotland
('Skogsruss')

Locality: Sweden–Gotland, Lojsta.

Colour and characteristics: Primitive characteristics. All shades of dun, black, brown, chestnut and grey. Straight face; large ears; short neck; good withers; long back trifle weak; sloping quarters; tail low-set; sufficient chest; hard legs and feet; mane and tail inclined to be sparse. Exceptionally hardy and quick, although inclined to be obstinate.

Height: 12 to 12·1½ h.h.
Weight: About 400 lbs.

The *Gotland* ponies or '*Skogsruss*' are bred chiefly on the Gotland island. They are descended from a very old breed, which ran wild in the forests. Nearly a hundred years ago a Syrian stallion was introduced and also an Oriental stallion. The ponies are in demand by small farmers and are also being specially bred now for pony trotting races. There is also a Swedish cold-blood trotter, the *North-Swedish*. (See p. 148).

Swedish Warm-Blood

Locality: Sweden – Flyinge.

Colour and characteristics: Bay, brown, chestnut and grey predominate.
Very good-looking horse of excellent conformation and disposition.
Courageous, intelligent and gentle, but slow to develop. Good, free action, first-class saddle-horse for show-jumping and three-day events.

Height: About 16·2 h.h.

The *Swedish Warm-blood* horse was originally based on *East Prussian, Hanoverian* and *Thoroughbred* blood. Even earlier Oriental and Spanish horses were used, and the breed is now fixed and has developed into a most useful, good-looking riding horse for all purposes. In Sweden, as well as representing their country in the Olympic games, they make a fine show in harness.

90

Fjord (Fjording)

The *Fjord* or *Westlands* pony is one of the few breeds of ponies or horses which even today bears a recognisable resemblance to his illustrious ancestors—the horses of the Ice Age, the wild horses of Mongolia. His characteristic colour is cream or yellow dun with a dark mane, tail and dorsal stripe; sometimes even the bands or stripes on the legs are to be seen. Some 2,000 years B.C. ponies were being bred in northern Europe and at a much later period the Vikings were keen horsemen and fond of horse-fighting. Today the *Fjord* pony is found in many north European countries, engaged in every kind of farm work. (See also p. 84).

Locality: West Norway.

Colour and characteristics: All shades of dun with dorsal stripe, black and silver mane and tail, often stripes on forelegs and hocks. Upright mane is characteristic (cut to shape). A square, compact, exceptionally well-muscled animal; small, neat head, wide between clear, dark, quiet eyes; big nostrils and strong jaws; very powerful neck that 'merges' into shoulders; no wither; short hard legs.

Height: About 13·1 to 14·1 h.h.

Northlands

Locality: Norway.

Colour and characteristics: Generally, but not always, dark, with full mane and tail. Extremely hardy, frugal. Small head; small pricked ears; eyes widely spaced; firm neck set on not too sloping shoulders; good barrel; firm quarters; iron-hard legs.

Height: About 13 h.h.

The *Northlands* pony is a very little known breed, similar to the now extinct Lofoten islands pony, and it belongs to what is generally termed 'the northern pony type'; they are considered to possess Mongolian-Tartar blood. They belong to the whole group of Baltic ponies (e.g., *Konik*) and to the group of 'Celtic' ponies (e.g., *Iceland, Shetland, Exmoor*). They are therefore descendants of *Equus przevalskii gmelini (Tarpan)*. If the photographs of the *Gotland, Exmoor, Huzul, Konik* and *Tarpan* are closely examined, the likeness will be seen. (See pp. 39, 40, 41, 89, 115).

92

Döle-Gudbrandsdal

Locality: Norway–Östlandet, Tröndelag and Trondheim districts.

Colour and characteristics: Mostly black and brown. Neat square head; crested neck; back inclined to be long, but strong, powerful shoulders and quarters; short feathered legs and profuse mane and tail, often sweeping the ground.

Height: Stallions 14·3 to 15·1½ h.h.

Weight: 1,200–1,400 lbs.

The *Döle-Gudbrandsdal* can almost be classed among the cold-blood horses, having been bred from heavy Danish horses as well as from *Thoroughbred* and *Trotter* stallions. It is similar to the *Fell* pony of Britain and the *Friesian* of Holland.

Two *Döle-Gudbrandsdal* mares and foals. (See previous page).

Döle Trotter

The *Döle Trotter* type is a mixed breed. Bred originally in the same way as its near relation, an introduction of trotter blood was later made. Stallions of the *Döle* breed have to undergo a test (as do all stallions of every breed throughout Europe, with the exception of Great Britain, although the actual test varies). Stallions are proved over 1,000 metres in 3 minutes.

Locality: Norway.

Colour and characteristics: Generally brown, black or bay. Conformation, through crossing, that of an active, very hard harness horse. Hard bone, good lungs; steady and enduring.

Height: About 15·1 h.h.

Peneia Pony

Locality: Greece–Peneia, Peloponnese.

Colour and characteristics: Most colours including bay, brown, grey and chestnut. Small Oriental type pony; exceptionally hardy and willing; frugal, strong worker.

Height: Varies considerably between 41 inches and 14·1 h.h.

Peneia, in the province of Eleia, Peloponnese, has a local breed of ponies which are used for farm and pack transport. They are very sturdy and economical. Stallions are used for breeding hinnies. The head-collar is of particular interest, the same type being in use some thousand years B.C.

Pindos Pony

Pindos ponies are bred in all the mountainous and semi-mountainous regions of Thessaly and Epirus; they are used for riding and light farm work. Farmers use the mares to breed mules. Ponies have been bred in Thessaly from ancient times and, as may be observed, they are of Oriental origin. The poet Oppian (*c.* 211 A.D.) mentioned three breeds of ponies—*Achean* (Peloponnese), *Thessalian* and *Thracian*.

Locality: Greece–Thessaly and Epirus.

Colour and characteristics: Often grey; dark colours. A hardy, strong mountain pony.

Height: 12 to 13 h.h.

Skyros Pony

Locality: Greece–Island of Skyros.

Colour and characteristics: Dun, grey, brown, etc. Small, fine-boned pony; worst points are not very good shoulders and cow-hocks.

Height: 37 inches to 11 h.h.

The small *Skyros* ponies from the Aegean island of that name remind one forcibly of the *Tarpan* group. The photograph shows a very young pony whose diminuitive size is probably due to sparse feeding. It is used locally to carry water and in the threshing of corn. Outside the island of Skyros, these ponies are kept to teach children to ride in the various riding clubs. This breed existed in classical times.

96

Iceland Pony

The ponies, like the people, migrated to Iceland in the 9th century from Norway, but later settlers brought Western Islands ponies with them. So the present-day *Iceland* pony is of mixed origin. There are two types for draught and riding; the latter have a distinctive action known as the tølt, which is a trotting amble. A stallion, Kinnskoer, from Sweden had a part in developing the breed. Many ponies (and people) died in the terrible winters between the 13th and 18th centuries, and in 1784 a great eruption destroyed a vast number.

Locality: Throughout Iceland.

Colour and characteristics:
Predominantly grey and dun; also dark brown and chestnut and occasionally black. Strong, sturdy, docile ponies of independent character, excellent sight and pronounced homing instinct. Riding gait is the amble.

Height: 12 to 13 h.h.

Viatka

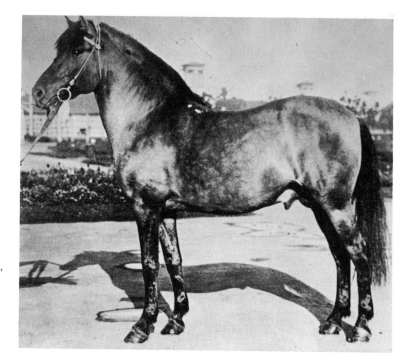

Locality: U.S.S.R.–Baltic States.

Colour and characteristics:
Dark colours. Plain head; fairly good conformation; hardy, frugal, fast; an honest, willing worker.

Height: 13 to 14 h.h.

The Baltic states have raised a number of native breeds based on the *Klepper* and *Konik*. The *Viatka* pony is an extremely useful all-round pony. Although somewhat larger, it resembles closely the *Konik* of Poland. Another very similar breed is the *Pechora,* or *Zemaituka,* of Lithuania, which is most enduring and hardy and able to cover forty miles a day on the simplest fare. This is the stallion Orlik.

This is a typical *Pechora (Zemaituka)* mare.

Pechora (Zemaituka)

Locality: U.S.S.R.–Baltic States.

Colour and characteristics:
Brown, palomino, dun with dorsal stripe. Medium-sized head; straight face; smallish ears; short neck and medium-straight shoulder; compact back and sloping quarters; hocks sometimes inclined to be weak. Hard, very willing, economical pony.

Height: 13·1 to 13·3 h.h.

Toric

One of the best known working or harness horses of the far north is the *Toric* breed—so named after the stud—and known earlier as the *Esthonian Klepper* and *Double Klepper*. There is a considerable amount of *Hackney* and *East Friesian* blood in this breed, which is used for all agricultural purposes. Although draught breeds, the *Toric* and the *Latvian* and *Lithuanian,* shown on the next page, are normally classed as warm-bloods.

Locality: U.S.S.R.–Esthonia.

Colour and characteristics: Chestnut and bay with white markings. Medium-sized head; strong muscular neck; low withers; short, broad, muscular back and loins; broad chest and rounded barrel; broad, long croup; short, strong legs; short cannon bone; well-developed joints and hard tendons; white hooves of medium size.

Height: Stallions 15·1½; mares 15 h.h. 8¾ inches of bone.

99

U.S.S.R.

Lithuanian

Locality: U.S.S.R. – Baltic States.

Colour and characteristics: Predominant colour bay, more seldom black and chestnut. Large head; long neck; high, long withers; straight back and loins; long croup and deep chest; sloping shoulders; strong legs with well-developed joints. Gait: walk and trot.

Height: Stallions 16½ h.h. mares 15·3½ h.h. 9 inches of bone.

Both the *Lithuanian* and *Latvian* breeds of harness horses are based on the *Zemaituka*. To obtain a heavier breed, the *Finnish Draught Horse* was used and later the *Swedish Ardennes* and *Oldenburg*. Great stress is now laid upon the pulling ability of the stallions, and tests are carried out, as they are in all northern European countries, to prove a stallion's capabilities before he is allowed to be used for stud purposes. For example, the stallion, Petsis, covered 2,000 metres with a load of 1,700 kg. in 17 min. 2 sec. The *Lithuanian* harness stallion was bred at Niemen and the *Latvian* stallion, Petsis, at Vidzemsk.

Latvian

Characteristics as above.

Don

Locality: U.S.S.R. – Budjonny Stud.

Colour and characteristics: Grey and other hard colours. In height, a retangular frame, showing much 'daylight' or appearing long on the leg; good, hard head and neck set into excellent shoulders; long, strong thighs. Horse of exceptional stamina.

Height: 15·1½ to 15·3 h.h. Average 8¼ inches bone.

The present-day *Don* has been improved from the old *Don* horse, a small, hard, active animal with a proportion of oriental blood. *Thoroughbred* and *Orlov* stallions were used to effect improvements recently, but as far back as the 18th century *Turkmene* and *Karabair* stallions were used. It is fundamentally a steppe horse from the regions of the river Don to the Caucasus mountains. The breed matures late, but is very hard. On one stud farm alone there are 1,500 head of horses. The *Don* mares are seen on the shores of Lake Sankul in the Kirghiz.

101

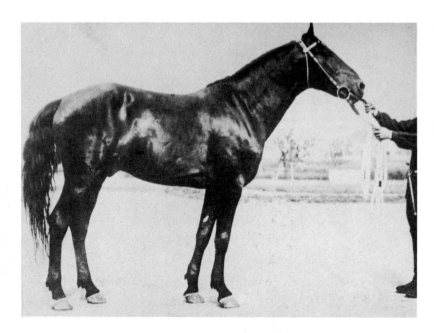

Kustanair

Locality: U.S.S.R.–Kazakh.

Colour and characteristics: No specific colour given. Very hard harness/saddle horse; much stamina and endurance.

Height: Stallions 15·2; mares 15·1 h.h. Just under 8 inches of bone.

The improved *Kustanair* horse is evidentally descended from the ancient *Kazakhs* strain. This breed has been improved by crossing with the *Don*. The nomad Kazakhs bred a useful, hardy horse capable of covering 40-60 miles a day on grass alone. The *Adayev* mare, seen below, comes from the southern Kazakh steppes.

102

A HIGHLAND PONY MARE. Here is a prize-winning Highland Pony mare, Mo'Run Geal Dileas, with panniers attached to her saddle. Her name means 'My faithful, fair beloved' and she belongs to Mrs K. Warren, New Calgary Stud Farm, Sussex. (*Photograph by the author*)

A PAIR OF HACKNEY HORSES. These two superb harness horses, Fairmile Satellite and Simonstone Sunspot, were competing in the open pair class at the Royal International Horse Show at the White City. Driven by Mr Stanley Hinder, they won this event for their owner, Mrs D. S. Hughes. (*Photograph by John Nestle*)

U . S . S . R .

Budjonny

Locality: U.S.S.R.–State Studs, Rostov area.

Colour and characteristics: Chestnut and bay, both colours with golden tint, occasionally white markings. Neat head with small ears on crested neck; good conformation; strong legs. An elegant, strong, warm-blood horse. Very fertile. Jumping ability in steeplechases, Olympic Trials, Concours Hippiques, etc.

Height: 15·3 h.h.

The *Budjonny* breed of horse is mostly a cross between the *Thoroughbred* and the *Don* horse and is a fairly recent evolution begun by Marshal Budjonny at the Army stud in the Rostov district about 25 years ago. They are kept in herds under the care of a groom.

Kirghiz

Locality: U.S.S.R.–Kirghiz.

Colour and characteristics:
Generally dark colours.

Height: Stallions 15½ h.h.
Mares: About 14·2 h.h.

The *New Kirghiz* is a comparatively new breed and is a cross between the native *Kirghiz* and *Don* or *Thoroughbred* stallions. These horses have remarkable stamina and are particularly suitable for work in mountainous regions, where they are often used for pack-transport.

Karabakh

Zaman, presented by the Government of the U.S.S.R. to Her Majesty Queen Elizabeth II, is a golden dun *Karabakh* stallion. These horses are mainly used for racing. Since his arrival in England Zaman has been at stud.

Locality: U.S.S.R.–
Karabakh Stud, Azerbaijan.

Colour and characteristics:
Golden dun, other colours,
with black points, black mane
and tail, sometimes black list,
white markings allowed.
These horses have small
heads; face is straight; small
muzzle with very open
nostrils; alert, intelligent eyes;
head is set on a well-
proportioned neck let into a
good chest, with good flat
shoulders; compact body;
good quarters; hard legs;
hard blue hooves.

Height: Average 14·1 h.h.

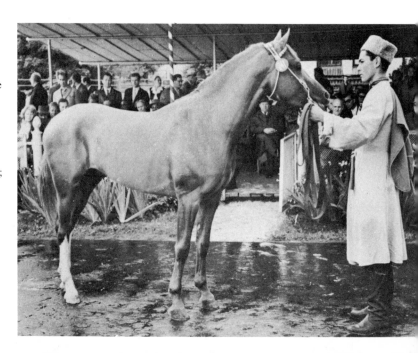

Karabair

Locality: U.S.S.R. – Usbek.

Colour and characteristics: Three types.
Most colours. Basic type (Pack/Harness/Saddle).

Height: 15·1 h.h.

Saddle type:
Height: 15·1½ h.h.
Heavy type:
Height: 15·2½ h.h.

The *Karabair*, which has influenced the *Don* breed, is an older breed of horse, of which there are apparently three types—an all-round horse, a riding horse and a heavier animal. It is bred in the Usbek district and is very often of a golden chestnut colour.

Another breed which comes from the Caucasus regions is the *Kabardin,* a very good, extremely sure-footed riding horse with *Turkmene* and *Arab* blood. It will carry its rider fearlessly over the narrowest of cliff trails and across turbulent mountain streams, and it possesses an excellent sense of direction. The breed is very fertile and is used to produce milk. An endurance test was made with a number of these horses of 47 days in the mountains in winter when they covered a distance of 3,000 km. without a single horse falling out (Landstallmeister Dr. W. Uppenborn: *Handbuch der Tierzüchtung)*.

Kabardin

Locality: U.S.S.R. –
Mountain areas of
Northern Caucasus

Colour and characteristics:
Generally bay. Strong
horse, with plenty of
stamina; very sure-footed;
hard tendons and tough
feet. Excellent sense of
direction; efficient
disposition; elastic action.

Height: About 15 h.h.

Lokai

Locality: U.S.S.R.–Tadzhik.

Colour and characteristics: No specific colour given. Strong, hard horse; well-muscled back and loins.

Height: About 14·3 h.h.

The *Lokai* is another 'mountain-bred' horse from central Asia. It is a very strong animal used as pack or riding horse. This is the stallion called Krasavets.

Jomud

Another breed capable of great endurance in a hot, waterless climate is the *Jomud*, closely related to the *Achal-Teké* and therefore descended from the *Turkmene* strains. They are used in harness and under the saddle.

Locality: U.S.S.R.–Turkmen.

Colour and characteristics: No specific colour given. Hardy, wiry horse with plenty of stamina and endurance.

Height: Stallions 15 h.h.; mares 14·2½ h.h.

Locality: U.S.S.R. – Turkmen, Kazakh, Usbek and Kirghiz.

Colour and characteristics: Golden dun, golden bay, grey; other colours occur. Light head with long face; large expressive eyes; large fine nostrils; neck long and thin and set high; long high withers; long back and loins; croup pronounced; narrow chest and not deep; flat ribs and long sloping shoulders; legs long; hard, strong tendons; hooves small with very hard horn. Lively temperament and sound constitution. Very fine skin covered with silky hair; mane and tail hair sparse. A pacer.

Height: About 14·2 to 15 h.h.

Achal-Teké

The *Achal-Teké* horse is bred in a number of provinces, and is a direct descendant of the very old *Turkmene* race (a name which covers a number of breeds such as the *Jomud*). The *Turkmene* is mentioned as a racehorse nearly 1,000 years B.C. and an interesting comparison may be made between the *Achal-Teké* stallion, Moro, and the *Persian Arab* stallion; the extraordinarily alert head carriage and stance is typical of this breed (p. 185). The *Achal-Teké* is a real horse of the desert, and is described as occasionally being spotted, striped and of golden dun colour. This horse has been known to cross 900 miles of desert without water to drink. Moro is shown on the next page.

109

The *Achal-Teké* stallion, Moro.

A group of *Achal-Teké* mares and foals.

Turkmene

Locality: U.S.S.R. – Collective Farm, Moshua, Ashkhabad.

Colour and characteristics: Brown, bay with golden tint, white markings; black, grey and dun with silver tint. Medium head, straight face, long neck; very high head carriage; fairly prominent withers; long back, pronounced croup and sloping quarters; flat ribs running up; iron hard legs. Of exceptional stamina and endurance; fearless, obedient, and very fast.

Height: About 15·1 h.h.

The *Turkmene* horse is of ancient origin and appears to have many points in common with the *Munighi Arabian*. The flow of blood probably extends both ways. The *Turkmene* horse *(Achal-Teké)* was valued for his speed 1,000 years B.C. and 30,000 Bactrian horsemen made up the cavalry of King Darius of Persia. The breeding of this horse is therefore of considerable antiquity.

111

Strelets Arab

Locality: U.S.S.R. – Tersk

Colour and characteristics: Three types – *Siglavy, Kuhaylan* and *Munighi.*
Generally chestnut, grey, etc. *Siglavy:* refined concave *Arabian* head;
large, prominent, expressive eyes; normal length neck, beautifully arched;
sufficiently pronounced withers; short back; rounded loins; oval croup;
chest not deep but with well-sprung ribs; long sloping shoulders; good,
hard legs. **Height:** About 14·3 h.h. *Kuhaylan:* Distinguished by their
strong constitution, hardiness and are not particular about their food.

Height: About 14·2 h.h. *Munighi:* Larger and possessing a greater speed
in racing. **Height:** About 15·1 h.h.

One of the best known of all Russian *Arab* breeds is the *Strelets Arab,* bred at the
Tersk State Stud near the Caucasus mountains. Bâbolna (in Hungary) and Crabbet
Park (in England) supplied a number of *Arabs* to this stud, and some from the Janow
Podlaski stud (Poland) are said to have been taken there.

112

Orlov Trotter

Locality: U.S.S.R. – 34 State Studs.

Colour and characteristics: Grey, black, and other colours. Long, thick-set, bony horse of good regular conformation. Large head with dark expressive eyes; arched neck on medium withers and very good muscular shoulders; strong back; broad moderately elongated croup; good legs and tendons, with a little feather on fetlocks. A show harness horse and racing trotter.

Height: 15·3½ h.h.
(*Note: Russian-American Trotter* – see next page – is a lighter but thick-set horse; same height).

The *Orlov Trotter* is probably the best known outside Russia of all the breeds of horses. The Orlov horse was evolved about 1777 by Count Alexis Grigorievich Orlov. The breed was produced by crossing with *Arab, Thoroughbred, Dutch, Mecklenburg* and *Danish.* The *Orlov* is a very handsome horse, rather Arabian in appearance, although he may stand up to 17 h.h. He was considered supreme as a *Trotter,* until the *American Trotter,* commercially developed for the purpose, ousted him from the position. A very great number of *Orlov Trotters* are bred in the U.S.S.R., particularly at the Moscow State Stud. There is also the *Orlov-Rostopschiner,* a particularly good sort of riding horse.

Métis Trotter

The racing trotter above, named Veterok, is considered to be one of the best of the very recent *Métis Trotter* breed – *Orlov* x *Standardbred*. In this new breed the very best trotting blood on both sides of the 'family' has been used. Trotting has become one of the most popular sports all over the world, and practically every country has trotting tracks. Below is a stallion of the type usually called *Russian–American Trotter*.

Locality: U.S.S.R.

Colour and characteristics: A new breed; characteristics of the *Orlov* x *Standardbred*. Those of the trotter in general.

Height: Average 15·3 h.h.

114

Locality: Great Britain,
Exmoor area of Somerset
and Devon; a few in
Continental Zoos.

Colour and characteristics:
Bay, brown, mouse dun, with
mealy muzzle and 'toad eye';
mealy belly and inside
thighs; dark points; in winter
a wiry coat, peculiar to the
breed.

Height: Mares not to exceed
12·2, Stallions 12·3 h.h.

Exmoor

The *Exmoor* pony of Somerset is by far the oldest of the native breeds for it was known of in prehistoric times, and later undoubtedly became the 'Celtic' pony, used as a pack-pony and in the war chariots of the Celts. Because of its antiquity, it is regarded by many people as indigenous, but this is not strictly correct because the ponies must have walked over the prehistoric land-way to the south-west of Land's End. The stallion Aclander is seen above and a group of mares with a foal below.

New Forest

Locality: Great Britain – New Forest area of South England.

Colour and characteristics: Any colour. Rather mixed breed from which a definite type is emerging. Large, Oriental type head: short neck; good shoulders and plenty of depth in the girth; drooping rather narrow quarters; very sure footed.

Height: 12 to 14 h.h.

Mention is made of ponies in the *New Forest* during King Canute's reign, and thereafter in old documents we have glimpses of ponies running in the Forest. A number of other breeds have been turned out in the Forest during the centuries and the 'Forester' is of rather mixed origin. It has become a fairly big pony and is most useful as a riding pony for all members of the family, being extremely quiet and willing.

116

Locality: Great Britain–
Dartmoor, Devon.

Colour and characteristics:
Preferred bay, black,
brown; odd colours
barred. A strong, good-
looking riding pony.
Small, well-bred head;
very small, alert ears;
strong shoulders, back and
quarters; full tail and
mane, tail set high; good
action, tough well-shaped
feet.

Height: Not exceeding
12·2 h.h.

GREAT BRITAIN

Dartmoor

The *Dartmoor* pony of Devon is found under similar climatic conditions as the *Exmoor* and is its neighbour geographically. The breed has had infusions of outside blood over the years. A number of herds run out on the moor, but there are also a number of private studs, and great efforts have been made to improve the *Dartmoor* pony into a really first-class children's pony.

GREAT BRITAIN

Locality: Great Britain – Westmorland and Cumberland.

Colour and characteristics: Black, brown, bay, sometimes with mealy nose. Strongly built, alert mountain pony. Full silky mane and tail; pony head with prick ears; strong muscular body; tail carried gaily; strong legs set squarely, with plenty of bone; heels covered in feather; open, round hard feet, blue horn.

Height: 13 to 14 h.h.

Fell

The *Fell* and the *Dales* pony share common ancestry, being descended from the 'Celtic' pony. They both acquired great fame in the 17th and 18th centuries as pack-ponies because they were the only means of transporting lead from the mines to the Coast. They were—and a few still are—used in the mines in Durham and Cumberland, and they have always proved their value to the Fell and Dales farmers for all purposes of work. The *Fell* ponies above have Windermere behind them. A typical *Dales* pony, below, is helping to bring feeding stuff to the sheep on a Durham farm.

Dales

Locality: Great Britain – Co. Durham and Northumberland.

Colour and characteristics: Jet black, bay, brown, occasionally white markings. Exceptionally strong pony. The head should be pony-like; neck short with straight shoulders; strong and muscular back and quarters; well-sprung ribs; tail not set high as is generally found in mountain and moorland breeds; feather.

Height: Up to 14·2 h.h.

Welsh Mountain

Locality: Four sections, Great Britain–Wales.

Colour and characteristics: SECTION A. Generally grey, brown, chestnut; no odd colours in any section. A small, well-bred riding pony of exceptional intelligence, courage and endurance. Slightly concave face; very soft muzzle like the Arab; small, prick ears; alert intelligent eyes; graceful neck on deep shoulders, marked by strong, short back; tail set high and carried proudly; short limbs; flat bone; hard, small feet. The foundation stock for Sections B, C and D.

Height: Not exceeding 12 h.h.

The *Welsh Mountain* pony has the oldest *recorded* history of the native breeds, as it goes back to Julius Caesar, who apparently founded a stud at Lake Bala, Merionethshire. From this time a certain, if small, amount of Oriental blood was used to breed up pack ponies from the native mountain pony. They are bred out on the hills and mountains (and, of course, in private studs) in a semi-wild state, having to endure all kinds of weather. Thus, hardiness and resistance to illness are bred in the ponies.

119

Welsh Pony

Colour and characteristics: SECTION B. The same as for *Welsh Mountain Pony*. A well-made riding pony; kindly temperament.

Height: Up to 13·2 h.h.

Colour and characteristics: SECTION C. Harness pony with cob characteristics; hardy, energetic, willing, economical.

Height: 12 to 13·2 h.h.

From the *Welsh Mountain* pony there have been developed the three other members of the Stud Book sections. Some *Welsh Mountain* pony blood has gone into the creation of the *Hackney* pony. The Section B *Welsh* pony *(above)* makes an ideal child's show pony with beautiful action. *(Below) Welsh* pony (Cob type). A very sturdy and attractive pony, endowed with enduring properties.

Welsh Cob

Locality: Great Britain – Wales.

Colour and characteristics: SECTION D. Bay, brown, black, roan, chestnut,
dun and cream. Small head, with small, prick ears; strong body
with deep girth; very powerful quarters and broad, generous chest;
tail well-set; legs short and strong, and clean with a little silky hair upon
the heels; should stand out, but not over too much ground; action is
active and the general outlook bold and energetic. (Heavier cobs are found
in various parts of Wales and in the South; a horse of considerable strength).

Height: Average 14 to 15·1 h.h.

The *Welsh Cob,* likewise descended from the *Welsh Mountain* pony, appears in song
and verse as early as the 13th century, when the Powys Cob, through the importation
of Spanish destriers (war-horses), first became famous as an all-round mount for the
knights serving King Richard I. It is exceptionally nimble-footed and strong, was
much favoured by farmers throughout the ages, and is still used as a harness and
riding cob.

121

Highland

Locality: Great Britain–Scotland. Two types.

Colour and characteristics: Dun with dorsal stripe, silver hairs in mane and tail or black points; grey, bay, dark brown and sometimes chestnut with silver mane and tail. The Mainland pony is exceptionally strong and well-made, docile and honest; neat, attractive head with intelligent, kindly eyes; short ears; powerful quarters and loins; deep chest; strong, short legs; flat bone; prominent tuft of feather at the fetlock joint; full mane and tail almost reaching the ground, but well carried; action free, straight and sure; natural paces are walking and trotting.

Heights: Mainland. About 14·2 h.h. Western Isles. From 12·2 to 13·2 h.h. and from 13·2 to 14·2 h.h.

The *Highland* pony was formerly divided into two types—the Mainland and the Western Isles. Although the latter was the oldest and purest-bred of the two, it is the former which won the day to be generally recognised as the *Highland* pony. These ponies are capable of carrying great weight—even the carcase of a deer—down the slippery slopes of the hill-sides; they were also much used by the crofters as general utility ponies.

122

Shetland

Locality: Great Britain–North Scotland and Islands.

Colour and characteristics: May be any colour including dun, blue dun, piebald and skewbald. Small, refined head, sometimes concave; small ears; small muzzle with open nostrils; large, kindly eye; profuse mane, often double, and tail sweeping the ground; in winter fine, thick coat; in summer fine and sleek; very gentle disposition; back is short, strong and deep through the girth; well-sprung ribs, good withers and sloping shoulders; legs are very hard, very short in the cannon bone; small, open feet; light, straight, airy action.

Height: Not over 10·2 h.h.; generally about 9·3 h.h.

The *Shetland* pony is of ancient origin, a native of the most northern islands–Shetland and Orkney. There it was used by the inhabitants for all working purposes. For its size the pony is considered the strongest of all the breeds. The breed is now to be found in many European countries, where it is invaluable for horticulturists; it is perfectly at home in America. The pictures show typical examples of *Shetlands*–Easter Joy taking Patricia Barham for a ride and the charming head of Harviestoun Suna. Compare these with *American Shetland* ponies (p. 236).

Locality: Great Britain and in many other countries throughout the world.

Colour and characteristics: Any colour and with white markings. At its best, one of the most beautiful horses, with excellent conformation. Refined head with big, intelligent eyes widely spaced; long, arched neck; pronounced withers, sometimes very high; sloping shoulders; short back; well-sprung ribs; generous quarters; croup high; tail well set; clean, hard legs, flat bone and knees, hocks well let down; tendons pronounced. Very fine, silky coat, under which muscles and small veins may be seen. Action free, great stride, showing speed.

Height: Varies. There are exceptionally good small horses, and first-class big ones. Sprinters: Generally 15 to 15·3 h.h.; Average: 16·1 h.h.

Thoroughbred

The breeding of the *Thoroughbred* began in England about the beginning of the 18th century with the importation of the Darley and Godolphin Arabians and the Byerley Turk, which were mated with native mares and Oriental mares. Eclipse, the most famous of all early *Thoroughbreds*, was foaled in 1764 and, through him and other *Thoroughbreds*, racing in England achieved world-wide renown. Horses were exported all over the world, and *Thoroughbreds* in every country owe their origin to the horses originally bred in Britain. The name is what it implies—thorough or *carefully* bred—and although the *Thoroughbred* has had a most beneficial influence on many other breeds, it is still, as breeds go, a very young breed.

Border Legend is a typical *Thoroughbred* sire of hunters, etc. As a three-year-old he won six hurdle races, and then for seven successive seasons he won shows under the Hunters' Improvement and National Light Horse Breeding Society Stallion Premium scheme. He was awarded a Premium five times, and was twice Champion.

124

Locality: Great Britain – Yorkshire.

Colour and characteristics: Bay, bay/brown, black points, permissible small white star and white hairs in heels and on coronets. Large, head, well carried on long neck; withers not too pronounced; strong, well-made body, longer than in most horses; hard, short, clean legs, 9 inches of bone below the knee. An excellent carriage horse with the added qualities of a good hunter.

Height: Desired 15·2 to 16 h.h.; sometimes taller.

Cleveland Bay

Before the days of coaches when merchandise, such as wool, cloth, corn and pots, were carried by pack on horses' backs, the travelling salesmen were called chapmen and so the horses then used became known as Chapmen horses. Later the Cleveland district of Yorkshire specialised in breeding good, strong horses for coach and agricultural work, and the '*Old Cleveland Bay*' was improved by two *Thoroughbred* sires, Manica (by the Darley Arabian), and Jalap (by Regulus, by the Godolphin Arabian). The economy, longevity and lasting qualities of the breed were recognised all over the world. Both the *Cleveland Bay* and the *Yorkshire Coach Horse*, which owed its origin to the *Cleveland Bay* and the *Thoroughbred*, were extensively exported and today there is a greater demand for *Cleveland Bays* than can be met. The *Cleveland Bay* mare seen above is Lady Fairfax.

125

Hackney Horse

Locality: Great Britain and U.S.A.

Colour and characteristics: Generally brown, bay, black and chestnut. Small head; large eyes; thick-set, crested neck; powerful shoulders (straighter than in a riding horse); muscled quarters with exceptionally strong hocks; compact body, barrel running up; tail set and carried high; good feet; action brilliant, extravagant; appearance energetic and full of fire.

Height: 14·3 to 15·3 h.h.

The *Hackney Horse* and the *Hackney Pony* are of the same breed; they have been sent all over the world. They originated from the *Norfolk Roadster* with *Thoroughbred* cross, but *Welsh* and *Fell* pony blood is also to be found in the *Hackney Pony*. Their uses today are mainly as show harness horses; their exaggerated knee and hock action, which must be level and even, is much admired. *Above* is Marden Midas, driven by Mrs F. Haydon; *below* is Hurstwood Starlight.

126

The *Hackney Ponies* seen here are Highstone Nicholas and Oakwell Sir James.

Hackney Pony

Locality: Great Britain.

Colour and characteristics: Generally brown, bay, black and chestnut. True pony type, with pony head; small prick ears; compact little animal with good shoulders and quarters; hard legs; good feet inclined to be narrow; action spectacular, fluid and energetic; hocks brought up under the body, high knee action; all movements should be true and exact.

Height: 12·2 to 14·2 h.h.

127

Spotted Horse

Locality: Great Britain recently and U.S.A.

Colour and characteristics: White, blue/red/chestnut, roan; silky coat with superimposed black or chocolate spots. Patterns are known as: blanket, harlequin, raindrop, polka dot, leopard spot, dollar spot, spotted rump, speckled. Silver hairs in mane and tail. Conformation very varied.

Height: Usually 14·2 to 15·2 h.h.

It is difficult to say in which country *Spotted Horses* originated, but their colour is probably very ancient, since they are depicted in early Chinese works of art. Beside the *Knabstrup* horses, a similar breed of *Spotted Horses*, called the *Appaloosa*, was developed by the Nez Percé Indians of central Idaho. Their coats are silky, sometimes white or partly red-roan with black or chocolate spots of different sizes, which can be felt with the fingers, as if they are superimposed. On the quarters the spots may be so close as to give occasionally the effect of a stripe; there is often much silver hair in the mane and tail. The Spotted Horse Society was revived in Britain in 1963. (See also under Denmark and United States).

Connemara

Locality: Republic of Ireland–Connaught.

Colour and characteristics: Dun with dorsal stripe and black points; grey, bay, brown/black with white markings. A compact, deep body; medium legs, covers much ground; generally neat head on good neck; good shoulders and quarters often sloping; clean, hard, flat bone. Docile, hardy constitution.

Height: 13 to 14 h.h.

The *Connemara* pony of Connaught has similar ancestry to the *Highland* pony, the original colour being dun with black mane and tail and a dorsal stripe. The Irish have always used them for many purposes, and the ponies have undoubtedly played a part in the development of the famous Irish hunter. In the middle ages Spanish blood was introduced and subsequent breeders both in Ireland and England used Arab blood to give the breed more refinement.

Irish Cob

Locality: Republic of Ireland.

Colour and characteristics:
All colours. Type is
disappearing. Strong, active
very hard horse; hard legs.

Height: About 15·2 h.h.

The *Irish Hunter,* like the *Irish Cob,* is a type—although the breeding of these horses has been an industry of the agricultural regions of Ireland for several centuries. Perhaps with more practical and scientific concentration, the hunter would have become an established warm-blood breed. These very good horses are descended from the *Connemara* pony, the *Irish Draught* horse and the *Thoroughbred.* Quite a number of international show jumpers are of the hunter type; they are courageous, sure-footed animals able to gallop on and stay. Below is Captain d'Inzeo on The Rock, bred in Ireland.

Irish Hunter

Locality: Republic of Ireland.

Colour and characteristics:
All colours; skewbalds
and piebalds are never seen.
Strong, well-made
horse; very hard legs,
good bone 8½ inches
below knee; generally
good, rather large feet;
good shoulders, with often
sloping quarters.
Excellent jumpers.

Height: Seldom under
16 h.h.

130

EUROPE: Cold-Blood or Heavy Draught Horses

BELGIUM. Belgian Heavy Draught; Belgian Ardennes; Belgian Country-Bred.

GERMANY. Rhineland Heavy Draught; Schleswig Heavy Draught; Niedersachen Heavy Draught; South German Cold-Blood (Noriker).

DENMARK. Jutland.

SWEDEN. Swedish Ardennes; North Swedish Trotter; North Swedish.

FINLAND. Finnish Universal; Finnish Draught.

FRANCE. Ardennes; Percheron; Trait du Nord; Seine Inférieure; Breton, Boulonnais; Poitevine.

U.S.S.R. Vladimir Heavy Draught; Russian Heavy Draught.

GREAT BRITAIN. Shire; Clydesdale; Suffolk Punch.

REPUBLIC OF IRELAND. Irish Clydesdale.

E U R O P E: Cold-Blood or Heavy Draught Horses

Heavy horses are found as original breeds in only a few European countries, although many other countries have imported these breeds and have 'bred them up' to standards of their own. Thus we have the original *Ardennes* (p. 152) of France, one of the oldest heavy breeds; the *Belgian Ardennes* and the *Swedish Ardennes* have come from this one type.

BELGIUM

Belgium was breeding Great Horses in the 11th century in Flanders and Brabant, where both climate and soil were ideally suitable. Not far distant in the Ardennes was a breed of small, active, heavy horse which was mentioned by Julius Caesar in 57 B.C. A frequent introduction of Oriental blood into the *Ardennes* produced an active war-horse that was much sought after. One of the best known modern Belgian breeds is the *Brabant* or *Belgian Heavy Draught* horse. These breeds go back to the famous Orange I. (See pp. 139-142).

GERMANY AND DENMARK

The *Rhineland* cold-blood horse of Germany shares the same ancestors as the *Belgian*. Fossilised bones of a prehistoric Rhineland horse have been found and early Roman writings record a breed of heavy, slow horses. Until 1876 various heavy breeds were introduced into the Rhineland, but after this date a definite type was established. At least thirteen other provinces in Germany followed suit and formed their own heavy horse breeds based upon the *Rhineland*.

The *Schleswig Heavy Draught* horse possesses a certain amount of *Thoroughbred* and warm-blood, and this is clearly seen in his lively disposition and free action and lastly by the fact that many breeders disputed as to whether the breed was really to be classed as warm-blood or cold-blood. The breed had to withstand the crisis of losing a greater part of its membership, but in 1949 there were sixty-seven stallions, double the number of ten years earlier, although nearly half a hand smaller! The *Schleswig* and the *Jutland* horse of Denmark have been bred on parallel lines. The *Jutland* is probably the older breed as it is mentioned in the 12th century.

England, Germany and France imported these horses during the Middle Ages, which explains why the chestnut stallion, Oppenheim LXII, with blaze and white hind fetlocks,* had such a tremendous success when used at stud.

The *Noriker* appears to be a native cold-blood breed and has its origins in the horse of the Roman province of Noricum, corresponding roughly to modern Styria and Carinthia. Although the horse was of primary importance in agriculture, a state stud was founded in 1769 to supply horses for the army and a number of warm-blood stallions were used to improve the breed—*Norfolk, Norman, Cleveland Bay, Holstein, Oldenburg, Hungarian, Thoroughbred* and *Arab*. Although there were two types within this breed—the *Oberländer* and the *Pinzgauer*, a heavy spotted horse—the breed is now united under the denomination *South German Cold-blood (Noriker)*. (See pp. 143-146).

SWEDEN

The *North-Swedish* horse is similar to the Norwegian *Döle* and although considered a cold-blood horse has many qualities of the warm-blood. The breed is descended from the native pony of the north; a likeness to the *Finnish* horse can also be seen. Having almost lost the breed through unsuitable mixed crossing, a revival was brought about in 1890 and today horses of the breed possess a better constitution than most draught horses. They are well-made and well-muscled with clean strong legs. One of the best stud farms is at Wangen. (See pp. 147-149).

FINLAND

Finland has two types of the one breed of horses—the *Finnish Universal* and the *Finnish Draught*. The original domestic horse shares the same features as the other members of the northern pony group. Cross-breeding with both cold-blood and warm-blood breeds has produced a light but sturdy small horse. This horse has the quietness, kindness and willingness of the former combined with the speed, liveliness and longevity of the latter. The *Universal* horse is used for transport and military purposes, and the *Draught* horse for agriculture and forestry. The breed is unfortunately decreasing. (See pp. 150-151).

FRANCE

France has the largest number of heavy horse breeds of any country in the world.

*Some authorities describe him as a *Suffolk Punch*, others as a *Shire*.

They vary from active but heavy cob types to cold-blood breeds. 'Statistics given in 1951 show that out of 2·4 million horses, about 1·5 million were heavy horses, out of 800,000 cross-bred probably the greater number were also heavy horses'.*

The most popular breed seems to be the *Breton*, which has spread over a number of districts where the soil is poor. The ancient indigenous breeds are the *Percheron*, which is decreasing and which has quite a lot of Oriental blood, the *Ardennes*, and the *Breton*, which has been bred for centuries 'with affection' and is indispensable for work of all kinds. The *Heavy Breton* differs considerably from the *Postier Breton* (p. 157) although they are both entered in the same stud book. Lastly there is the *Boulonnais,* which is said to owe its descent to the *Arabs*** (p. 158) used by Caesar's legions which were stationed along the French coast before the invasion of Britain. Other infusions of *Arabian* blood are said to have come from the horses of the returning Crusaders and during the Spanish occupation of Flanders.

In fact, the *Boulonnais* does remind one of the *Arab* with its small, expressive head—unusual in heavy horses—its fine skin, its good bone and clean legs, its elegance and stamina and hard, active disposition. Although practically extinct there is also a small *Boulonnais.*

The *Comtois* breed is said to have originated in the German horses imported by the Burgundians; they were mentioned by Publius Végèse in the 4th century. They had many uses and were to be seen at tournaments, and were used as carriage horses. The Swiss use the *Comtois*, bred in the Doubs and Belford regions, to improve their *Franches-Montagnes* horses.

The *Auxois* draught horse is a derivation of the former *Bourguignon*, raised in the 'granary of Burgundy'. This included the whole south-west of the Côte d'Or, part of Avallonais, part of Saône et Loire, Epinac-les-Mines, Autun and Lucenay l'Evêque. These horses take their place between the *Ardennes* post horse and the Northern draught horse.

The *Trait du Nord* originated in French Hainault from which he spread south and west. It is now bred chiefly in Aisne, Somme, Oise, and parts of Seine-et-Marne. Caesar praised these horses, which were often used for Roman cavalry purposes.

Quite the opposite in conformation—if one is looking for elegance—is the *Poitevine*, which is almost unknown outside its own locality. These are also known as *Mulassiers*, for they are used solely to breed the huge Poitevine mules which are in great demand and are used in great numbers in the Americas. The *baudet du Poitou*—a large jackass—is crossed with the *jument mulassière poitevine*. The *Poitevine* breed of horse has a northern origin (Holland, Denmark, Norway) and it appears to have all the faults of

*There was no such breed as *Flemish* or *Flanders*, but the ancestor of the *Belgian Heavy Draught Horse* was already much in demand as a 'weight breeder'. A number were imported to Britain and as already stated, they helped to found the *Rhineland* as well as other heavy breeds. The *Friesian* was also imported in numbers.

**There were no *Arabs* as a breed at this period.

134

conformation that a good horse–should not have—large heavy head, thick ears, short neck set on a straight shoulder, long barrel and coarse legs. And they are not even very good working horses! The purpose of the mares is to breed strong, first-class mules and this they appear to do in the most satisfactory manner. (See pp. 152-159).

BRITISH ISLES

Great Britain has three breeds of heavy horses of her own—the *Shire, Clydesdale* and *Suffolk Punch*; the *Percheron* is imported from France. The *Shire* undoubtedly has its origins in the Lincolnshire and Cambridgeshire fenlands, in the native mares and the imported Great Horses of the Middle Ages and, subsequently, in the *Old Black English* horse. 'To move weight, you require weight' was at one time a maxim, and the *Shire* was bred for draught power. The breed became the agricultural horse of the Midlands around 1878, but it has enjoyed a comparatively short period of prosperity, since with the advance of mechanization the heavy horse is regrettably fast disappearing from the counties of which he is so much a part. At one time it was fashionable for *Shire* horses to have a lot of feather on their legs. The impracticability of this, when the animals are worked on wet heavy soil, has caused breeders to try to breed out the tendency to some extent—but even so the *Shire* has more hair than any other breed.

The *Clydesdale* is very similar but rather lighter and belongs to southern Scotland and latterly to Ireland. In 1682 the Duke of Hamilton imported a number of Flemish stallions and these added weight to the native Lanarkshire breed. Both *Cleveland Bay* and *Shire* blood was later used. Like the *Shire*, the fetlock joints of the Clydesdale are said to be occasionally weak, although latterly experts are satisfied that there is a great improvement in this condition, which at the most applied only to some animals. A great number of *Clydesdales* have been exported all over the world.

The *Suffolk Punch* is the oldest of the heavy breeds. In the 16th century writers referred to the 'old breed', which is traceable back to 1506. The chestnut stallion, Chrisp's Horse (1760), is the founder of present-day lines. *Norman, Jutland* and *Belgian* horses were imported, and comparison with the two former breeds and the *Suffolk Punch* is worth while. Another sire, Blake's Farmer, was a trotting horse and Barber's Proctor, the old Shadingfield horse foaled in 1798, was descended from Eclipse! The *Suffolk Punch* was one of the earliest to be used in road coaches or wagons. They are ideal working horses, capable of drawing considerable loads, active, clean-legged, with good dispositions and long-lived.

At one time teams were 'matched' for draught and were forced to pull very heavy loads and even standing trees; to do this the *Suffolk* would get down on his knees. Unfortunately this so-called sport ruined many willing horses.

There were also *Norfolk* cobs and *Suffolk* cobs—short-legged, punchy animals. (See pp. 160-163).

135

UNION OF SOVIET SOCIALIST REPUBLICS

There are a number of heavy breeds of draught horses in this country, beside the *Vladimir* and *Russian Heavy Draught Horse* (p. 164). All the heavy breeds are made up from cold-blood horses bred in the West, such as the *Belgian, Shire* and *Suffolk Punch*.

The *Lithuanian Heavy Horse* is a native of Lithuania and is crossed with the *Swedish Ardennes*. Average height is 15·3 h.h. The *White Russian* harness horse comes between the warm-blood and cold-blood breeds; this has been crossed with *Döle, Norfolk, Breton, Brabant* and even *Arab*. Standing only 15 h.h., these horses have great stamina and are very economical feeders, doing well on potatoes and green food. The *Woronesch* harness horse, bred in the Woronesch district, is really the improved *Bitjug* horse—a cross with *Trotters* and harness horses.

We have classed the three Baltic States breeds—*Toric, Latvian* and *Lithuanian*— among the warm-bloods.

THE ANCIENT ARDENNES BREED. These hardy cold-blood horses come from the mountains of the Ardennes and belong partly to France and partly to Belgium. This specimen of the breed is Max, owned by Herr Willi Manderfeld, of Lösheim/Eifel in West Germany. (*Photograph by the author*)

A PAIR OF GREY PERCHERONS. These powerful and handsome draught horses, either grey or black in colour, originated in France and are said to have Arab blood in their pedigrees. Now they are to be found in many countries, including the United States. (*Photograph by the author*)

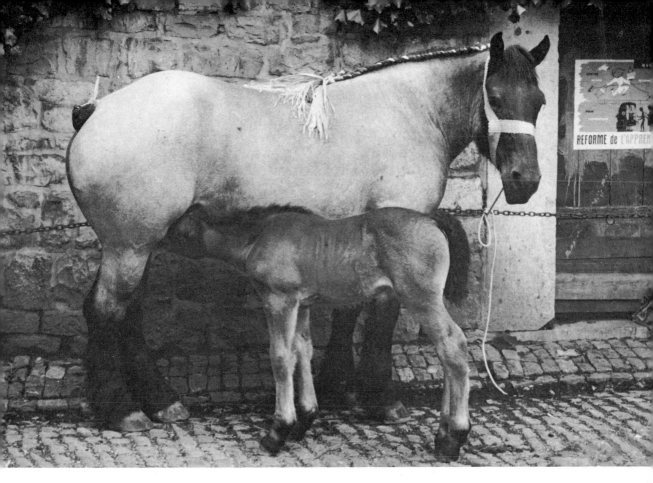

Belgian Heavy Draught

Locality: Belgium – Brabant.

Colour and characteristics: Often sorrel, dun, red-roan. One of the heaviest draught horse breeds – exceptionally strong and willing worker. Generally small, well-shaped head on good neck; massive shoulders and quarters; compact, weighty body; well-muscled, short legs; feathered fetlocks. Combines action and elegance with weight and activity.

Height: Up to 17 h.h.

The *Heavy Belgian Horse* is considered by some authorities to be a direct descendant— most likely through the even older *Ardennes*—from the diluvial horse of Quaternary Europe. It possesses one of the most ancient colours—sorrel or red-roan—and is a most able and willing draught-horse. In the middle ages horses of this breed were exported to many other European countries where they had a great influence on many well-known cold-blood breeds.

139

A group of
*Belgian Heavy
Draught* horses.

One of the best
specimens of the
*Belgian Heavy
Draught* breed.

Belgian

Ardennes

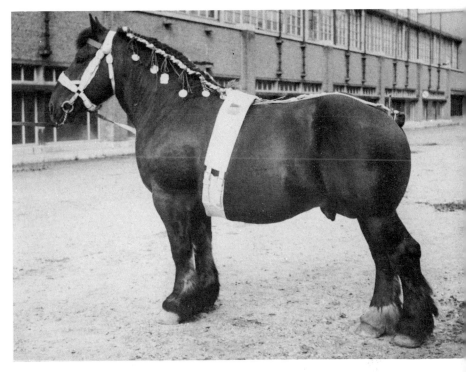

Locality: North-east Belgium.

Colour and characteristics: A lighter type of the Draught Horse. Has the same blood.

Height: About 15·3 h.h.

The *Ardennes* horse is found in the sandy districts of north-eastern Belgium. It is considered to be a 'middle-heavy type', and both photographs should be considered side-by-side—the one having put on so much fat for show and the other in working condition. The *Ardennes* today has the same blood as the *Brabant*, but does not have so much quality; the medium light *Brabant* horses are known as *Ardennes*. There is a close relationship between the Belgium *Ardennes* and the Swedish *Ardennes*.

141

Belgian Country Bred

Locality: Belgium.

Colour and characteristics: All colours, generally sorrel, dun, red roan. Characteristically useful working horse.

Height: About 16 h.h.

The Belgian Country Bred horse is usually produced by using an *Ardennes* or *Heavy Draught* stallion on half-bred mares. It proves to be a very useful general working horse.

Rhineland
Heavy Draught

Locality: West Germany. Horses of this type are found in many other Provinces under breed names. Bred on same lines as the *Belgian Heavy Draught*.

Colour and characteristics: Sorrel, chestnut, chestnut-roan with flaxen mane and tail, red-roan with black mane and tail. An exceptionally heavy, square horse. For his size a neat head, set on a massive, crested neck; tremendous shoulders and rounded muscular quarters; strong, short, feathered legs; low to the ground, giving great traction power.

Height: 16 to 17 h.h.

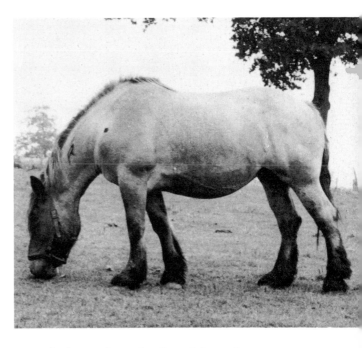

The *Rhineland* or *Rheinish-German Heavy Draught* horse is to be found in a dozen different forms and names all over Western and Eastern Germany. The author is of the opinion that, if it could be traced, the origin of the *Rhineland* horse, like the *Belgian*, goes back to the *Ardennes* and further to the diluvial horse of prehistoric times. It has very much in common with the *Belgian* horse whose ancestors it shares. The Stud Book goes back to 1876. In the *Niedersachen Heavy Draught* horse we see the same points, which include conformation and colour: usually shades of roan, from cream to chestnut and red, sometimes with black points, mane and tail and sometimes chestnut.

Niedersachen
Heavy Draught

Locality: West Germany – Lower Saxony.

Colour and characteristics: Chestnut, bay brown, sorrel or roan. Very similar by breed to the *Rhineland*. Low to the ground.

Height: Around 16 h.h.

Schleswig Heavy Draught

Locality: North-west Germany – Province of Schleswig-Holstein.

Colour and characteristics: Chestnut predominant. Similar breed to the *Jutland*. A heavy cob-type horse, very low to the ground. Plain, large head; heavy crested neck and almost no wither; inclined to long barrel and flat ribs and to flat, soft feet; very docile, willing disposition and also active.

Height: About 15·3 h.h.

In the north of West Germany, the *Schleswig Heavy Draught* horse holds sway. It is nearly related to the *Jutland* horse of Denmark. Both breeds owe something to the *Suffolk Punch* stallion, Oppenheim LXII, which was imported in 1860. There is certainly a very close resemblance between all three breeds.

Locality: Formerly Roman province of Noricum. Austria (called *Pinzgauer*)–Salzburg, Tyrol, Karutin, Steiermark, etc. Germany (called *Obërlander*)–Upper and Lower Bavaria.

Colour and characteristics: Bay, brown, chestnut, dun, spotted and skewbald. Heavy head on thick, short neck; straight, loaded shoulders; short ribbed, broad chest; broad cleft quarters with tail set low; short, feathered pasterns and good flat hooves.

Height: 16 to 16·2 h.h.

South German Cold – Blood (Noriker)

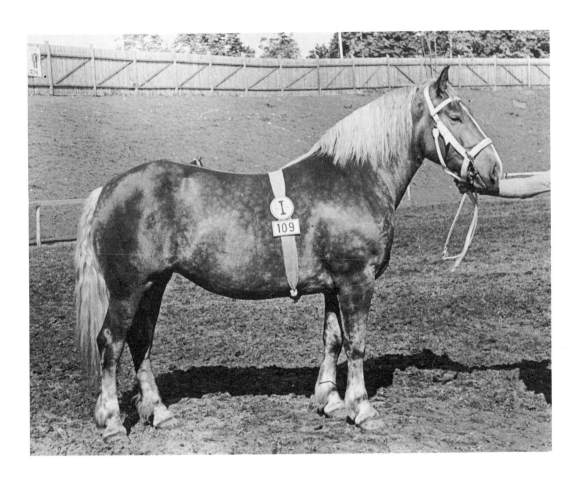

The *Noriker*, or *Pinzgauer*, is a cold-blood horse, of the type of a small cart-horse. It is used for farm-work in many parts of Bavaria and Upper and Lower Austria. This horse has a very ancient history, being bred in the province of Noricum by the Romans and the stud was founded in the Land Salzburg. This breed is also much used in other mountainous countries of Southern Europe, where horses of this stamp and weight are needed. The *Pinzgauer* 'Tiger-spot', a spotted horse, used to be very much in demand. This is a fine example of a *Noriker* mare.

145

DENMARK

Jutland

Locality: Denmark – Jutland and Fünen.

Colour and characteristics: Originally black and brown, today usually chestnut. A fairly compact, short-legged animal with feather (which breeders are trying to eliminate). Joints could be stronger and harder.

Height: About 15·3 h.h.

Weight: 1500 to 1800 lbs.

The *Jutland* horse is nearly related to the *Schleswig* (p. 144). It is a heavier type of draught horse and was originally bred on the island of Jutland by crossing with *Suffolk Punches, Cleveland Bays,* and *Yorkshire Coach* horses.

Swedish Ardennes

Locality: Central and southern Sweden.

Colour and characteristics: Generally brown and black. Strong, hard, quiet working horse; compact conformation and low to the ground; very little hair on legs; open blue hooves.

Height: 15·2 to 16 h.h. **Weight:** 1200 to 1600 lbs.

The *Swedish Ardennes* horse belongs to one of two heavy breeds, and has been bred from imported *Ardennes* and *Belgian* horses. It is a very useful animal, energetic, a good feeder and has a long life. The other heavy breed, and one which is not so generally well-known, is the *North Swedish* horse which is nearly related to the Norwegian *Eastland* horse; it is highly thought of for its easy temperament and usefulness.

North Swedish Trotter

Locality: Sweden.

Colour and characteristics: This is the only cold-blood trotter in the world; it has also been called the *Nord Hestur*. Usually chestnut or brown.

Height: About 15·2 h.h.

The *North Swedish Trotter,* Plurus, is one of the best horses to be seen on Sweden's trotting tracks. He has a record of 1·31,6 over a kilometre. At sixteen years of age Plurus is still active as a racing trotter.

A good example of the *North Swedish* horse.

North Swedish

Locality: Sweden–Wangen, Norenberg and Umea Agricultural School.

Colour and characteristics: Dun with black points, brown, chestnut, and black with white pasterns. Medium-sized horse with deep body and long, straight croup; clean legs correct in position; strong, large joints; strong skeleton and well-developed muscles.

Height: Average: Stallions 15·2; mares 15·1 h.h.

The *North Swedish* horse originates from ancient Scandinavian native horses and is first cousin to the Norwegian *Döle*. The main stud is at Wangen. It is a medium-sized, not too heavy horse, with deep body, clean, correct legs and of a sound constitution. It is very long-lived and appears to be immune to many equine diseases. A very energetic, active horse, it finds employment in agriculture and forestry and in the army.

Finnish Universal

Locality: Finland.

Colour and characteristics: Generally bay or brown; black, which used to be common, is disappearing; white markings allowed. General purpose horse weighing on an average 541 kg. (1193 lb.).

Height: About 15·2 h.h.

A *Finnish Universal* stallion.

There are two types of the one breed of Finnish horses—the *Finnish Universal* and the *Finnish Draught* horse, which is the smaller of the two. They possess features of both cold-blood and warm-blood horses; they are very quiet, kind and willing to pull, and these qualities are combined with speed, liveliness, courage and longevity. These horses are descended from importations of foreign breeds and the local native pony which is found in the countries along the Baltic coast. Trotting is an exceptionally popular sport; there are 10,000 amateur drivers and trainers and 800 trotting clubs.

A *Finnish Universal* trotter.

Finnish Draught

Locality: Finland.

Colour and characteristics: As *Finnish Universal.* Medium draught horse, weighing an average 576 kg. (1270 lb.).

Height: About 15·2 h.h.

Finnish Draught horses are capable of the hardest work on the farms and in the forests.

151

FRANCE

Ardennes

Locality: Eastern France – From the Thierache pastures to the Jura, from the Paris valley to the Rhine.

Colour and characteristics: Bay, chestnut, sorrel and roan. Strong, muscular body, deep chest; short, very hard, lightly feathered legs; easy, quick action; gentle temperament.

Height: Stallions: 16 h.h.; mares: 15·3 h.h.

There are two other quite different types of horses which share the distinction of belonging to the *Ardennes* breed. In the opinion of the author, it is the French *Ardennes* which is the true and probably the almost direct descendant of the diluvial horse. This breed was mentioned by Roman chroniclers and undoubtedly formed the basis for the breeding up of the Great Horses of the middle ages. Originally a small draught horse on short legs, when well done the horse rapidly assumes the characteristics of a much heavier animal.

152

Percheron

Locality: France – Department of Sarthe, Eure-et-Loir, Loir-et-Cher, L'Orne.

Colour and characteristics: Grey or black. Small, fine head, wide between eyes; long, fine ears, lively eyes; good, well-made neck, on good wither; deep chest, strong back and well-proportioned quarters; clean, hard legs; open, hard hooves.

Height: From 15·2½ to 17 h.h.; average 16·1 h.h.

In the district of Perche, to the south-west of Paris, one of the most important breeds of horses in France—the *Percheron*—is to be found. In very early times the breed was a cross of Oriental with Norman horses, but later heavier horses were used. The breed is not always 'even' and we show here a heavy and light pair of *Percherons*. For heavy horses they have remarkable stamina in the trot and can average 35 miles a day. They are energetic and active in all gears and have been widely exported to America, Australia, Great Britain and Russia.

Trait du Nord

Locality: France – Aisne,
Pas-de-Calais, Somme,
Seine-et-Marne.

Colour and characteristics:
Very strong, heavy horse,
with deep chest and girth and
low to the ground; great
resistance to rough climates;
docile and easy. Local
variations are *Auxoise* and
Comtoise.

Height: 15 to 15·3 h.h.

Seine Inférieure

Locality: Central France.

Colour and characteristics:
Bay, brown, sometimes roan.
Useful heavy draught horse.

Height: About 16 h.h.

The *Trait du Nord* is first cousin to the *Ardennes*, although bigger and heavier. This horse is able to pull heavy loads in deep going. He is very sturdy and hardy, putting up with the worst changes of climate. Usually bay or chestnut in colour. Similar, although not so heavy, are the *Auxoise, Comtoise* and *Seine Inférieure*. All these horses are used for agricultural work in France.

154

A PAIR OF SUFFOLK PUNCHES. These two fine horses, in their show tack and gleaming brasses, were taking part in an annual British National Ploughing Match, held in November at Keswick Hill Farm, near Norwich. Suffolks are clean legged. (*Photograph by F. G. Dawson*)

EQUUS PRZEVALSKII PRZEVALSKII POLJAKOFF MARE AND STALLION. Here are Walski and Poljakoff in the Rotterdam Zoo. Their direct ancestor, *Equus przevalskii*, is considered to be the ancestor of all living breeds of horse; they are the true wild horse of the Altai Mountains of Mongolia. There are specimens at Whipsnade and in many other zoos. (*Photograph by the author*)

Breton

Locality: Three types. France – Brittany, Finistere, Côtes du Nord and in the Midi.

Colour and characteristics: Chestnut, bay, red roan and chestnut roan; latter colour not much in demand, but horses of this colour are considered to be among the best. *Postier Breton:* An extremely compact, short-legged animal with an elegant head on a well-crested neck; almost clean-legged; energetic action and constitution.

Height: 15 to 16 h.h.

Draught Breton: Conformation not so compact, less active, hardy and with stamina. **Height:** Average 15·2 h.h. *Breton (Corlay):* Typical compact mountain pony.

There are commonly three types of *Breton*—the *Postier Breton,* the *Draught Breton,* and the little known *Breton (Corlay).* All are fairly clean-legged and are bred in various parts of Brittany. The *Postier Breton* is a square, strong, active, punchy horse, with a resemblance to the old *Suffolk Punch,* which is not extraordinary as both Norfolk and Hackney blood were used up to the 1914 war. The *Draught Breton* is also of a squarish conformation, having been developed more along the lines of the *Boulonnais, Percheron* and *Ardennes,* which blood is found in both types. Usual colours are chestnut, chestnut roan, bay, and red roan. Black is extremely rare, and it is said that the chestnut roans have the most quality, although they are not as sought after as one might think.

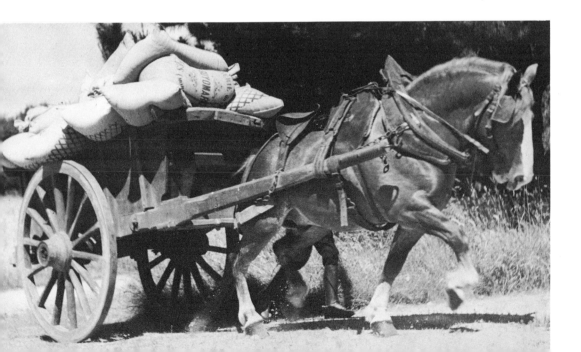

Boulonnais

Locality: France–Departments of the North.

Colour and characteristics: Grey. Characteristic small head, reminding one of the Arab; broad chest; powerful quarters; double croup, of medium conformation; clean legs often with flat hooves; exceptional action. Two types: very heavy and medium.

Height: Up to 16·3 h.h.

The *Boulonnais* is considered to be one of the best heavy breeds in France and is of excellent conformation. They are founded on the ancient heavy horse of northern Europe and, so it is said, on the Oriental horses imported by Julius Caesar before his invasion of Britain. Later *Arab* blood was again frequently used. They have very neat small heads, short backs, hard, good bone, a lively disposition with much stamina. There used to be a smaller *Boulonnais,* but this has practically disappeared. The 'baskets' prevent the horses nibbling at the corn they are cutting.

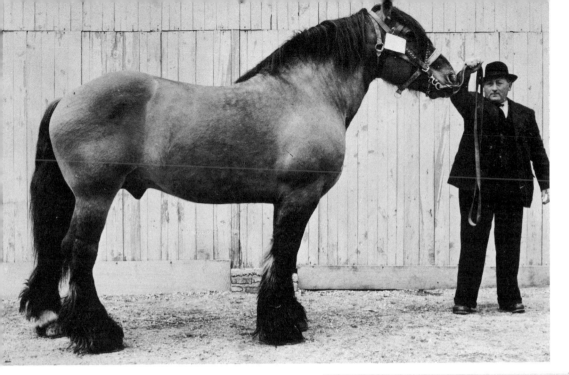

FRANCE

Poitevine

Locality: France–Landes district, especially Poitou.

Colour and characteristics: Usually dun. Large, long body; heavy head, with thick ears; often straight shoulders and sloping croup; unremarkable feathered legs; large feet.

Height: About 16·3 h.h.

Outside its own locality the *Poitevine* horse is scarcely known, but it plays a most important rôle in the breeding of the very large mules which have proved themselves time and again to be of great value. They were originally brought to the Marais Vendéens and Poitevins from Norway, Denmark and Holland by the Dutch who went there to drain the land. They have characteristic dun coats, large long bodies, heavy heads and thick ears, with very large feet, on account of being raised on the marshes, and are usually of a slow, dull disposition. Normally, the *Poitevine* mares have one object only—to breed mules to the *baudet Poitevin*, a large jackass, standing 16 h.h.

159

Shire

Locality: Great Britain–Shires.

Colour and characteristics: Black, brown, bay, grey and chestnut; at one time piebald and skewbald. Much white hair often from knee/hocks to fetlocks. Blaze or other white marks on face. Strong, heavy horse. Lean head, sometimes concave face, long, lean ears; slightly arched, long neck set on powerful, oblique shoulders; good round barrel and rounded loins.

Height: Average 17 h.h., some stallions reaching 17·3 h.h. Mares an inch or two less.

Weight: 2,425 lbs.

The *Shire* horse is a breed about which much discussion has raged. Its nearest ancestor was the *Old Black English Horse* of Lincolnshire and further back there was the Great Horse of Chivalry, which came from Flanders and other north Continental regions. On the other side there were native English mares, particularly written of in the 16th century. They are used in the Fens and Shires for all kinds of heavy agricultural work.

160

A fine team of
six black *Shires*.

Clydesdale

The Border land of south-east Scotland has produced the *Clydesdale,* which closely resembles the *Shire*. Indeed, about one hundred years ago pictures show almost the same sort of animal, although it may be argued now that the *Clydesdale* is a little more leggy. These horses are used for draught work of all kinds; they are active and of an easy disposition.

Locality: Great Britain – South-West Scotland and Ireland.

Colour and characteristics: Bay, brown, black, grey, rarely chestnut, with much white on face and legs and sometimes body. Broad, flat face, large nostrils, clear intelligent eyes; long, well-arched neck springing from oblique shoulders; high withers; short back; well-sprung ribs; muscled quarters; legs straight and directly under the shoulder; hind legs also straight with point of hock turned inwards rather than outwards; hard feet. An active courageous horse of friendly disposition.

Height: About 16·2 h.h.

Suffolk Punch

Locality: Great Britain – East Anglia.

Colour and characteristics: Chestnut of all colours, yellow, red, liver, gold, copper, dark and light; sometimes faint star. Quiet, kindly disposition. Elegant, short head; powerful, muscular, compact body on short, hard legs with almost no feather; wide chest and powerful shoulders; withers unremarkable. Great drawing ability; can trot.

Height: About 16 h.h.

Weight: 2,205-2,425 lbs.

The *Suffolk Punch* has evolved as a fixed breed during the past two hundred and fifty years in the Eastern Counties of England. In earlier times it was known as the 'old breed', but there is little doubt that it has the same forebears as the old *Norfolk Roadster*, which was a most useful cobby type. The *Punch*, so named because of its 'punchy' look, was used to pull the earliest road coaches. It works in all gears—a term used to describe a good working horse. A great number have been exported.

Irish Clydesdale

Locality: Republic of Ireland and Northern Ireland.

Colour and characteristics: Bay, brown, with white legs and white face/blaze; sometimes white hairs on body. Much feather. Has weight, size and activity; exceptional wearing qualities of legs and feet (see Great Britain).

Height: 17 h.h.

The *Clydesdale* originated in Scotland, but is now widely bred in Ireland, where horses are still much in demand for farming and agricultural use. A fine pair of Irish-bred *Clydesdales* may be seen here. *Clydesdale* horses have been exported to Australia, South Africa, Canada, the United States, South America, Italy, U.S.S.R. and Austria.

163

Vladimir
Heavy Draught

Locality: U.S.S.R. – Districts of
Vladimir, Ivanov, Tambov, Kostroma
and Moscow, and in the Tartar
Republic.

Colour and characteristics: Hard colours.
Well-made, hard working/harness
horse; very sound constitution;
energetic temperament and good action.

Height: About 15·3½ h.h.

Russia has imported a number of heavy horses from other countries. The *Vladimir* breed was based on *Ardennes*, *Percherons*, *Suffolks* and *Cleveland Bays*, and in 1910 *Shire* blood was introduced. It is an energetic horse, with good action and constitution. Great worth is laid upon the stallion's ability, when he is 'tested', to draw certain heavy weights.

Predominant colour of the *Russian Heavy Draught* horse is chestnut, bay and roan. It is not particularly large, but is economic for all farm work. The breed is based upon the native *Ukraine*, and crossed with *Swedish Ardennes*, *Percherons*, *Belgian* and the *Orlov Trotter*. It is distinguished by remarkable pulling power and fast gait at the walk and trot.

Russian
Heavy Draught

Locality: U.S.S.R. – Ukraine, Udmurt,
Kirovograd, Archangel and Vologda.

Colour and characteristics:
Predominating colours chestnut, bay,
roan. Short, thick-set, hard horse;
small head; massive neck of medium
length; broad, muscular back; short,
powerful loins; sloping croup; short
legs with hard hooves. Lively
temperament; light, free movements.

Height: Average 14·2½ h.h.

ASIA

MONGOLIA. *Equus przevalskii przevalskii* Poljakoff.

CHINA. Chinese Pony.

TIBET. Native Tibetan.

INDIA. Country-Bred.

INDONESIA. Sumba; Sumbawa; Sandalwood; Java; Timor; Batak; Bali.

TURKEY. Native Turkish Pony; Kurdistan Half-Bred; Karacabey.

PERSIA. Persian Arab; Darashoori (Shirazi); Jaf; Tchenarani; Turkoman.

POLO PONIES. Turkmene Pony; British Pony.

ASIA

Asia is the largest continent; it reaches beyond the Arctic circle and extends almost to the equator. It contains about one third of the whole of the dry land and one twelfth part of the whole surface of the globe. The climate is as extreme as it is possible to imagine, with the land varying from the frozen north with its mountains, forests and tundras, the torrid deserts, steppes and vast mountain areas in the centre, to equatorial jungles and islands in the south.

MONGOLIA

Mongolia has long been considered to be the world's chief theatre of evolution and the discoveries of the Central Asiatic Expeditions have confirmed this opinion. In the west Gobi desert, the skull of a tiny mammal, possibly the condylarth, was found. This is probably the earliest known mammal and, according to Dr. Gaylord Simpson (*Horses*), was the ancestor of 'most or all of the later and recent hoofed mammals', and a number of remains have been found in the United States.

The Great Gobi desert is a large tract of sand, stones and sparse vegetation. Saltweed, similar to that which often grows on sea-shores, and saxaul trees growing to about eighteen feet high, form occasional small woodlands. The saxaul has a juicy bark, which serves as a water reservoir, and in May has small yellow flowers that become a circular fruit in September.

On the western borders near the range called Tachin Schara Nuru—horses of the yellow mountains—are found the last remnants of the wild horses of Mongolia— *Equus przevalskii przevalskii* Poljakoff. They live now as they did most probably in the Pleistocene age. Civilization is encroaching on their grazing, and more particularly on their water holes, and the horses are being driven further and further back until they too may reach extinction.

These horses were discovered by the explorer, Colonel N. M. Przevalsky, in 1881. They are considered to be the part ancestors of all breeds of horses, although naturally in hundreds of thousands of generations and varying climatic conditions, no breed can claim direct descent.

Specimens of these prehistoric horses may be seen in many European and American Zoos. They stand from 12·1 h.h. to 14·1 h.h. and their colours range between dun, red dun and brown dun, with light bellies and mealy eyes and noses which become

166

lighter with age. A healthy wild horse annually changes the hair of its coat, tail and mane (which is upright), but at different times; they have dorsal stripes, often stripes on the neck and withers, and stripes on the legs. They are rarely tamed, but have been known to breed with Mongolian ponies.

A *Przevalskii* mare carries her foal 328-343 days; they are often covered at two years old, but usually breed every two years. They mature late, but live as long as thirty-four years. It is estimated that about forty *Przevalskii* horses may still be found wild in Mongolia, and hunting has been forbidden by the Mongolian and Chinese Governments. There are some hundred of these horses in Zoos, and the number is increasing. A stud book is kept, dating from the earliest Hagenbeck transports in 1901.

The Mongols have no form of agriculture, but raise great herds of horses (and cattle, sheep and camels) as do their neighbours, the Buryat Mongols, and other tribes. The *Mongolian* pony is a direct descendant of *Equus przevalskii przevalskii*. It occupies a most important place in the scheme of living because of its tremendous stamina and endurance; it is said to beat the *Arab* for hardiness. (See p. 172).

CHINA AND TIBET

The *Mongolian* pony is exceptionally fast over short distances and in China flat races are held for them. They are found in considerable numbers all over eastern Asia: bigger ponies are found in the north. The same sort of ponies are found in Tibet, although many are odd-coloured instead of varying dun colours, and in Spiti, Bhutan and Yarkand. A similar type is the *Hokaido* pony of Japan. (See pp. 173-174).

INDIA

Country-bred ponies of India, and the Manipur and Kathiarwari ponies, show traces of the same origin with more or less Oriental blood, as do the animals of Burma, Malaya and Indonesia. Although these latter types are far from pure—obviously stallions and mares of different breeds have been imported from time to time—they still clearly show a marked *Mongolian* influence. P. 176 shows a dancing pony of Sumba, 'Island of the Sandalwood Pony', with all the characteristics of his ancestor, *Equus przevalskii przevalskii* Poljakoff. (See p. 175).

INDONESIA

Indonesia, made up of groups of 3,000 islands, is indeed a land of horse-lovers, as the inhabitants live in close relationship with their ponies. They are indispensable in a roadless country, with poor grazing entirely dependant upon the rains. Everything rotates round the ponies, and ponies may be said almost to rule the islands.

167

Small ponies trot tirelessly in tropical heat, between the shafts of laden 'sados', the local carts. The local sport of throwing the lance at full gallop against opponents is practised on a sort of polo ground by the local rajahs and chieftains; the game comes to an end only when one side has no more riders.

The best *Sandalwood* ponies are used for racing in Sumba and Sumbawa. They have *Arab* heads, hard joints, good girth and fine coats—which most of the other ponies have not got. The races begin with a flying start over 4-5,000 metres, and in spite of the speed and the heat, the ponies finish neither sweating nor winded. Bits are not used and neither are saddles; bridles are made of plaited leather with hard nose-pieces. The same equipment was used in Central Asia some 2,000 years B.C.

Mares are selected from the islands and are sent to imported *Arab* stallions standing in the former Dutch stud at Minankababau, Central Sumatra, which is now organised by the government. Colts and fillies are then returned to the islands with the object of improving the stock. In a world where horses and ponies are dying out, it is good to know that in this part of Asia they are on the increase. (See pp. 176-181).

THE ARABIAN HORSE

According to a German authority, Dr. Zorn (*Pferdezucht*), 'the origin of the *Arab* is not clear, but the pure-bred *Arab* is a descendant of the *Tarpan*. Lipping believes that the *Arabian* horse is a cross between Central Asiatic horses (southern type) with horses of Altai-Mongolian descent (northern type)'.

Unfortunately a number of other Oriental breeds of horses have been called *Arabs*, when they are really *Barbs*, *Syrians* or *Turks*. Some authorities regard the original home of the *Arabian* as Libya, in north-east Africa, or Persia, but quite possibly Turkmen is their 'cradle'. Indeed, the Persians themselves maintain that the *Persian Arab* is the oldest known domesticated breed in the world.

Horses of this stamp were depicted some 2,000 years B.C. and are known to have been used, for war-chariots and riding, by the armies of the ancient Asiatic kingdoms. Pictorial comparison should be made between the *Tarpan*, and the *Achal-Teké*, the *Persian Arab* and the *Darashoori*.

Through the mares, there are five important lines and eleven families with individual pecularities and characteristics. These are: *Kuhaylan el Adjus*, *Siglavy* (both spelt in many different ways), *Habdan*, *Hamdani* and *Obajan*. The *Munighis* or *Maneghis* of Syria, Iraq, India, Egypt, Turkey and Europe are of a different type, considered to be ideal as racehorses. The Darley Arabian, one of the ancestors of the *Thoroughbred*, was a *Munighi*. The *Kuhaylan* is regarded as a masculine type, the *Siglavy* feminine.

The earliest records of horses in southern Arabia appear in 400 A.D. when two hundred *Cappadocian* (small Asiatic horses) were sent by Constantine the First to the Yemeni princes. About this time the Saracens and Thamuds appear on the scene

168

as mounted horsemen from Central Arabia.

Because of the lack of water—every drop had to be carried by camel—the only place where horses could be bred was the Nejd highlands, with the exception of a few wealthy nomadic tribes who owned a small number.

When Mohammed came into power during the 7th century A.D. he realised immediately the immense value of horses, both for his own armies and for the Arab people in general, and thus the horse became part of their social and religious world. From this period then, the desert-bred *Arab* has been pure-bred, and is known as *Élite-Arab* or *Original Arab*; and throughout the centuries the Bedouins have taken the greatest care in their choice of breeding material. 'The mares were selected for their endurance in long hunts or sorties covering great distances in the most difficult country when only the strongest survived. The stallions were chosen for their beauty, conformation and intelligence'.*

These horses are famed for their kind disposition, patience, trust and qualities of observation and also for their hearing, sense of direction and memory. Dr. Zorn, in *Pferdezucht*, tells the story of a man who thought he recognised his two horses, one an *Arab*, stolen during the war and removed some distance. He demanded their return and the judge ordered the horses to be present at a given place. When the man called his *Arab* by name, the horse pricked his ears and, neighing with pleasure, rushed up to his real owner, who regained both horses.

The head of a pure-bred *Arab* is one of its chief characteristics and the *Arab* breeder looks first to the head, then the hindquarters and then the legs. The horses were bred to withstand the extreme temperatures of the desert, hunger, thirst and sand-storms. Unfortunately, the breeding of the desert *Arabian* has decreased very much during recent years.

The action of these horses is light and graceful with a long stride. His natural gait is the canter, covering much ground, and the trot is generally inferior. Special qualities are stamina and endurance over long distances. Endurance records are 644 km. (390 miles) in five days and nights; 300 km. (180 miles) in two days and nights; and 100 miles in fifteen-and-a-half hours.

Many pure bred *Arabs* are grey or not quite pure grey (dappled or flea-bitten), but other colours are found, although black is rare. All pure-bred *Arabs* have a metallic bloom on their coats. Dr. Flade, in *Das Araberpferde*, points out that the true *Arab* type is kept only under the right (for him) conditions of feeding, such as he finds in the Nefud district of the Nejd. When grass is scarce the horses are fed with dried dates, dried camel and goat meat, locusts and possibly fresh vegetables such as carrots. Both young and older horses are given camel's milk during the spring. Neighbouring countries such as Egypt, Syria and Turkey must rely on lucerne and clover (green and as hay), barley, millet, dates, chaff and, where they can be grown,

* *Handbuch der Tierzüchtung: Rassen Kunde.*

169

green maize and carrots.

He adds: 'Other studs in Europe and America are forced to feed their *Arabs* differently, and such food in many cases leads to a change in conformation and type. The quality and amount of pasture plays a very important part. Since the value and quantity of the food ration often exceeds that of the chief breeding district (Nejd) animals thus reared grow bigger and lose certain interior and exterior qualities typical of their breed'.

Far more could be written here, and indeed has been written by other authors, on the *Arabian* horse. The breed has its own stud book in every country where it is bred and it is hoped that Egypt will issue an international stud book. As readers will have seen the breed has tremendously influenced other breeds all over the world.

There are a number of pure-bred *Arab* studs in Europe, Asia, Africa and the United States of America. I can mention only a very few from a considerable number of important studs. In England, the Crabbet Park Stud, Sussex, begun by the late Lady Wentworth, was one of the most famous, and horses from this stud have influenced many lines in other countries. Other studs are at Janow Podlaski, Albigowa, Michalów and Nowy Dwor in Poland; Tersk in the Caucasus, U.S.S.R.; Topoliancky in Czechoslovakia; Radautz and Bâbolna, in Hungary; Marbach and Weil, in West Germany; Jerez de la Frontera (where the *Carthusian* horses are bred) and Moratalla in Spain. In the United States are the well-known Kellogg Ranch, Pamona and Al Marah Studs, and there are a number of others which are equally important.

YEMEN

There are three recognised blood lines in the Yemen *Arabian* breed—Amran, Kawlan and Jaufi. Horses are ridden only by the King, Princes, officers of the State and the cavalry. They are bred at the royal studs of Dhamar, Yerim, Muran, Sanaa and Ma'baa; and also in the Jaufi district.

There are two types—the generally well-known *Arab* and a heavier *Arab*, standing about 15 h.h. The King's personal mount is of the heavier type and that rare colour, black, with three white fetlocks and a star; he is also very fast. Both types are exceptionally hard with great staying power. Horses are fed on small quantities of oats, maize, barley and durrah. Where possible, good quality mountain hay and seradella is included in their diet. In spite of the extreme heat, they are watered only once a day. Their action is the walk and canter and a kind of tipple-trot.

All well-bred horses carry their pedigree in a small leather *etui* around their necks. The Yemenis are devoted to their horses, which are treated according to the rules of the Koran, in which one reads that the number of a man's sins shall be forgiven him according to the number of grains of corn in his horse's manger.

170

ASIA

TURKEY

Turkey first appears in equine history when in the 14th century B.C. a historian wrote the earliest treatise in Hittite on horse management. And Turkey is still a land of horses, having well over a million used principally in agriculture, the army, as saddle horses and for pack transport and draught purposes. The native breed is the *Kurdistan* pony, and mares of this breed have been crossed with *Arab* stallions to produce an improved breed which is economical to use.

The Turkish state studs use *Nonius* stallions (see p. 58) to obtain larger horses. The most important breed of warm-blood horses are *Karacabey* and they are bred in the stud of that name. Pure-bred *Arabs* and *Nonius* horses are bred at six other studs. The *Syrian Arab* is an Oriental breed which has its origins around Aleppo, Baghdad and Damascus. (See pp. 182-184).

PERSIA

It would seem that the old *Turkoman* horse of Anatolia has much in common with the *Mongolian* pony of Upper Asia, but for many centuries the breed has been crossed with *Arabs* and other Oriental breeds. *Jaf* horses are bred in Kurdistan, and the *Darashoori*—better known perhaps as the *Shirazi*—are the most popular riding horses. (See pp. 185-188).

THE POLO PONY

This is the most convenient place to write about polo ponies. Polo, or 'pulu', is Tibetan for ball. Polo ponies are a type, and various breeds of horses or ponies have produced the type of active quick and handy pony needed to play the game. Polo is said to be the oldest ball game in the world and probably originated in Persia, where it was played before 500 B.C. The Persian poet, Firdawsi (935 A.D.), describes a game between Persian and Turkish teams.

It was popular with many east Asiatic peoples and was played on smaller ponies in India, Tibet, China and Japan. On the 'roof of the world', in the Pamirs, the game is called 'guibosi'. As we have shown, most of the Asiatic countries could breed exactly the right sort of hardy, nimble pony, which, when trained, was quite valuable. America, too, has produced some first-class ponies.

The game was introduced into England from India by officers of the 10th Hussars in 1859 and the United States took up the game keenly some twenty years later. (See pp. 189-190).

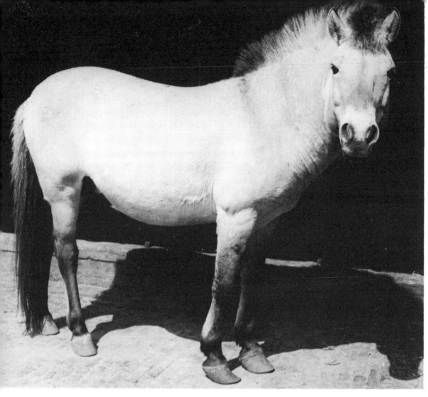

Equus Przevalskii Przevalskii Poljakoff

Locality: Mongolia – Western borders of Great Gobi desert. In Zoos at Askania Nova, Crimea, and in European countries and America.

Colour and characteristics: Shades of dun, ranging from cream to red; belly often lighter; usually dark points with zebra stripes on forearm, hocks and gaskins; dorsal stripe; upright mane; tail sparse.

Height: Between 12·1 and 14·1 h.h.

Equus przevalskii przevalskii Poljakoff, the wild horse of the Mongolian steppes, exists in much the same form today as it did in the Ice Age. These horses were discovered by the explorer, Colonel N. M. Przevalsky, in 1881. They are considered to be part ancestors of all breeds of horses, although naturally, in thousands of generations and in varying climatic conditions, no breed can claim direct descent. They have been decimated by hunting and encroachments on their native haunts, and there are thought to be only about 40 specimens left in the wild state. About a hundred are kept in Zoological Gardens in Europe and America, where they are now increasing. They have their own stud book.

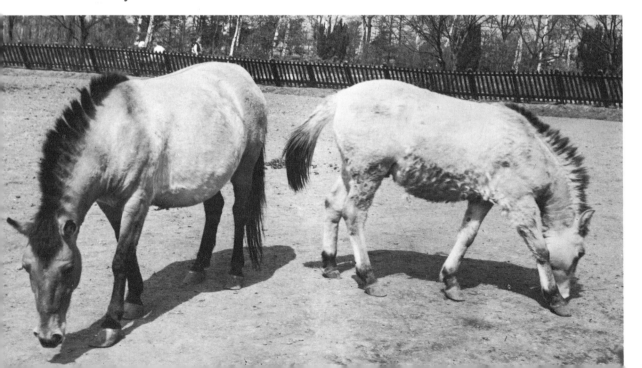

Chinese Pony

Locality: In most districts of the Chinese Republic.

Colour and characteristics: All colours; dun predominates with dorsal stripe and often black points. Compact and hardy of not particularly good conformation. Is a close relative of the Mongolian pony.

Height: In the north of Mongolia, about 13·1 h.h.; East Mongolia and China, 12 h.h.

The *Chinese Pony* can hardly be regarded as a breed, since ponies of this type are to be found in many countries of the Far East such as Mongolia and Korea; similarities occur also in the *Hocaido* pony of Japan, the *Sandalwood* pony of Siam, etc. The ponies are near-relatives to the Mongolian wild horse and are known to have inter-bred since early times with the domesticated ponies of China. These hardy, economical little ponies are used for all purposes including racing, and over short distances are said to be faster than the Arab. (*Handbuch der Tier Züchtung*).

173

Native Tibetan

Locality: Tibet.

Colour and characteristics: All colours including dun. Hard, strong, active pony, useful for all purposes.

Height: About 12·2 h.h.

There is little to be said of these *Tibetan* ponies except that they are descendants of domesticated Chinese and Mongolian ponies. The Dalai Lama kept a number (some of which are seen below), as did other wealthy Tibetans. It has been said that there exists a very much smaller breed similar to the *Shetland* pony, but accurate information is difficult to obtain.

Kathiawari and Marwari Ponies

Locality: India–Provinces of Kathiawar and Marwar.

Colour and characteristics: Any colour, including piebald and skewbald. Country-bred, with considerable admixture of Arab blood, shown by characteristic inward pointing of tips of ears; often long mane.

Height: About 14·2 h.h.

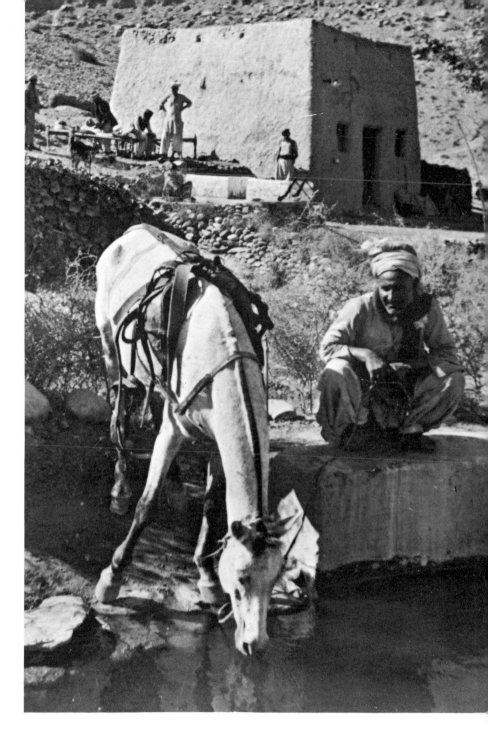

The *Kathiawari* and *Marwari* ponies are very similar, being small, tough and hardy like most 'country breds' in India. In the foothills of the Silwaliks, a number of prehistoric remains of horses have been found, and it is quite likely that horses or ponies were 'at home' in India long before they found their way into Europe.

175

Sumba

The dancing ponies of Sumba are the pride of their owners. They dance, with bells attached to their knees, to the rhythm of tom-toms. They are carefully judged on their elegance and lightness, and their eyes appear to grow bigger and to glow as they rival each other in the tempo of the dance. A small boy usually rides the ponies, while father gives exact directions to the pony by means of the lunge rope.

Locality: Indonesia–Islands of Sumba and Sumbawa.

Colour and characteristics: Most usually dun with dorsal stripe, dark mane and tail. An ancient primitive type. Exceptionally hardy, intelligent and willing.

Height: Varies, about 12·2 h.h.

176

Sumbawa

Characteristics as *Sumba*.

It is impossible to say when ponies were first brought to the Indonesian islands, but as some ponies resemble the Chinese or Mongolian domesticated ponies, it is quite likely that the Chinese brought them here in very early times. The Portuguese and Dutch are also said to have imported ponies. The islands now seem to have their own types. The *Sumba* and *Sumbawa* ponies are very agile and are used to take part in the national sport of throwing the lance. Particularly noticeable is the fact that the ponies are ridden in bitless bridles.

Locality: Indonesia –
Islands of Sumba and
Sumbawa.

Colour and characteristics:
Most colours. Usually
small, fine heads; large
clear eyes; deep chest;
very hard legs and tough
feet. Fine coats, fast
and active.

Height: 12·1 to 13·1 h.h.

Sandalwood

The *Sandalwood* pony is better bred than those usually seen in Indonesia. They have small heads rather like the Arab, clean joints, a good front and a soft, shining coat. They are used for racing without saddles and, although the distances are often 4-5,000 metres, the ponies rarely sweat or show other signs of distress. These ponies got their name because the biggest export from Sumba was sandalwood and ponies; they are still considered the most valuable ponies in Indonesia.

178

INDONESIA

Java

Locality: Indonesia – Island of Java.

Colour and characteristics: Most colours. Untiring pony of not very good conformation; often cow-hocked; possesses an astonishing willingness.

Height: About 12·2 h.h.

The *Java* pony is a little larger and stronger than thoses on some of the other islands. They are used in the two-wheeled 'sados', which are filled to capacity with people or goods. In spite of tropical heat they willingly pull their heavy loads.

Timor has its own breed of ponies, used by local 'cowboys' who catch the cattle with lassos. The *Timor* ponies are quite extraordinarily agile for their very small size.

Timor

Locality: Indonesia – Island of Timor.

Colour and characteristics: Usually dark colours. Small pony of great endurance; robust, docile and very agile.

Height: About 12 h.h.

INDONESIA

Batak

Locality: Indonesia – Island of Sumatra.

Colour and characteristics: Most colours. Common type of pony, frugal and docile.

Height: About 12 to 13·1 h.h.

Sumatra also has its own breed of ponies, the *Batak* pony. They have been carefully bred for many years in proper studs. The mares are carefully selected from some of the other islands and *Arab* stallions have been imported to help to improve the breed. The young stock is then dispersed, by the Indonesian government, to the islands to help to improve breeding there.

180

Bali

Locality: Indonesia – Island of Bali.

Colour and characteristics: Generally dun with black dorsal stripe, dark mane and tail. Strong, sturdy, frugal pony.

Height: 12 to 13·1 h.h.

Bali ponies are not only ridden but, like the *Sumbawa* ponies, are often employed for pack purposes; they are used for gathering stones from the sea to build walls, etc. Sometimes the manes are cut, but usually not; in this case when the mane remains upright it is a sure sign of their Mongolian blood. Comparison can be made with *Equus przevalskii przevalskii* Poljakoff (see p. 172).

181

Native Turkish Pony

Locality: Turkey–Sivas.

Colour and characteristics: Grey, bay or brown. Of ordinary, good
conformation; plain head and thick neck; short body; good bone.
Exceptionally hardy, enduring and willing.

Height: 14 to 14·2 h.h.

At the last count in 1951 there were over one million horses in Turkey. They are
generally used in agriculture and are a usual means of transport. Most of the studs are
organised by the state, and one of the most important is the Karacabey stud, where the
useful *Karacabey* horse is bred for remounts and agriculture (p. 184). At the same
stud *Arabs* and *Nonius* are bred, and there are six other studs where *Arabs* are also bred.

TURKEY

Kurdistan Half-Bred

Locality: Turkey–
Kurdistan.

Colour and characteristics:
Any colour. Medium head;
thin, medium length neck;
rather flat-chested, with
fine legs and joints. Very
docile, hardy and good doer.

Height: 12·3 to 14·1 h.h.

The greater number of Turkish horses like the *Kurdistan* are used in agriculture, as 80 per cent of the population are farmers. Half-bred horses are also used for transport and as pack animals. The Republic of Turkey has done a great deal to encourage and improve breeding. *Below,* team of horses and cows threshing wheat.

183

Karacabey

Locality: Turkey—Bred in the Karacabey stud.

Colour and characteristics: May be any solid colour. General purpose horse of good conformation and endurance.

Height: Around 15·3 to 16·1 h.h.

The *Karacabey* is the one stable native horse in Turkey, although several other races are bred in this country. It is used as a light draught horse in agriculture and as a cavalry horse. There are seven state studs; Karacabey, Cifteler, Konya, Cukurowa, Sultansuyu, Karaköy and Altundere.

184

Locality: Persia.

Colour and characteristics: Shades of grey, bay, etc. Conformation
as far as can be ascertained: *Siglavy*. Elegant appearance; fine, muscled
compact body; typical concave Arabian head; widely-spaced ears; very
broad forehead; large, dark eyes; wide, open nostrils. Best gait is the
canter.

Height: 14·3 to 15·1 h.h.

Persian Arab

The *Persian Arab* is one of the oldest known domesticated breed of horses in the world.
It is thought that these horses were brought into Persia some 2,000 years B.C. Thus
the breed is some 1,500 years older than the *Arab* of Arabia. They are, however,
strange as it may seem, still descended from the *Tarpan (Equus przevalskii gmelini)* and
the *Mongolian* wild horse *(Equus przevalskii przevalskii* Poljakoff). But thousands of
years of love, care and judicious breeding have turned them into one of the most
beautiful specimens of the equine race.

185

Darashoori
(Shirazi)

Locality: Persia – Province of Fars.

Colour and characteristics: Grey, chestnut, bay, brown. Oriental saddle horse, similar to the *Arab*. Easy gaits, docile disposition.

Height: About 15 h.h.

The *Darashoori* (*Shirazi*) are bred in the State of Fars, in southern Persia, north of the Persian Gulf, not far from the supposed cradle of mankind. They are a popular breed for riding, and they possess very fine coats, mane and hair.

Jaf

The *Jaf* horses come from Kurdistan, while the *Tcherarani* and the better known *Turkoman* are bred in the north of Iran, south-east of the Caspian Sea. They are good horses to ride on the plains, but not so useful in mountainous country. These horses are never shod in their own part of the country, but near Tehran, the capital, or where the earth is harder, it becomes necessary to shoe them.

Locality: Persia–Kurdistan.

Colour and characteristics: Grey, chestnut, bay, brown. Oriental saddle horse. Hard, wiry, active desert horse, with very hard, tough hooves.

Height: Varies.

PERSIA

Tchenarani

Locality: North-West Persia.

Colour and characteristics:
Oriental saddle horse rather
resembling the *Kuhaylan
Arabian*. Considerable
endurance at the canter.

Height: About 15 h.h.

Turkoman

Characteristics as above.

Polo
Ponies

Locality: Great Britain,
U.S.A., the Argentine,
India, etc.

Colour and characteristics:
Any colour.
Characteristics are
according to the country of
origin and speed of game.
Long, flexible neck; strong,
short back; good girth;
muscular quarters; hard
legs, with hocks well let
down; courageous and
obedient disposition;
action fast, handy,
responsive.

Height: 14·2 to 16 h.h.

Polo has become an international game, played in countries all over the world. It is one of the world's oldest games, having been played in Persia before 500 B.C. There are records of the game in Byzantium and later in Japan and China, whence it spread to Tibet and India. In the 19th century British Army officers stationed in India began to play the game and, in its modern form, it soon spread to the United States, various South American countries and elsewhere. On 'the roof of the world', in the Pamirs, the Tajiks play a game similar to polo which they call 'guibosi'; again they are mounted on a *Turkmene* strain of horses.

189

Champion polo pony stallion, Grey Star.

The *Polo Pony* has been bred from several of the native pony breeds, including *Connemara* and *New Forest*. Argentine ponies have also been introduced, so have ponies from India, Pakistan, etc. and, mated with a small *Thoroughbred,* the *Polo Pony* has evolved. *Below,* a game of polo at Roehampton.

AFRICA

EGYPT.   Egyptian Arab.

LIBYA.   Libyan Barb.

ALGERIA AND MOROCCO.   Barb.

CAMEROON REPUBLIC.   Fulani Horse.

NIGERIA.   Nigerian Horse.

BASUTOLAND.   Basuto Pony.

AFRICA

Africa is one of the continents belonging to the Old World. It is connected with Asia by the Suez isthmus and is separated from Europe by the Mediterranean Sea; it is bounded on the west by the Atlantic Ocean and on the south by the Indian Ocean. There are a number of important mountain ranges and two great deserts, parts of which are covered with scrub. Nearly three-quarters of the total area lies within the tropics.

Africa has always been sparsely populated with breeds of horses, although both the ass and zebra abound in certain areas. Up to the present it is not known with absolute certainty if this continent ever had any indigenous breeds of horses.

S. Ruy d'Andrade, the Spanish authority on horses, suggests that similar ponies to the *Garranos* of Portugal appear in north Africa, equatorial Africa, Guinea, Togoland and Somaliland. In fact, a careful study of the specias *equus* in Africa seems long overdue. The tsetse fly has always been one of the greatest menaces to the horse.

The Hyksos (the Shepherd Kings), who conquered Egypt in about 1680 B.C., probably introduced the horse chariot and possibly horses into the African continent. At least we may assume with certainty that Oriental horses were brought into Africa by the Hyksos.

EGYPT

Although Egypt bred horses of Oriental type many centuries B.C., the first real introduction of *Arabian* horses from breeding centres in Arabia began during the 14th century when the ruling dynasty, the Mamelukes, used pure-bred *Arabs* to improve the saddle horses bred from their native mares.

El Zahraa and Ein Shams became the chief studs for breeding *Original Arabs*, because they were both situated so near the desert, yet with every opportunity for obtaining green maize and lucerne from the Nile Delta. The climate, too, is exactly right and under excellent stud management both studs have produced some of the most typical and valuable desert *Arabians*. The type is called *Kuhaylan* or *Siglavy* and pure bred horses have been sent all over the world. Races are held in Heliopolis, near Cairo, to test these animals, and about 800 horses are in training there.

A game called 'tahtib' is played on horseback and horses are specially selected as foals and trained to take part in what is really mounted fencing. At the Feast of

192

Luxor horses also take part in traditional 'dancing'. The horses are said to be extremely sensitive to the aids and to the music, and much patience and skill is needed to train them correctly. (See p. 195).

LIBYA, ALGERIA AND MOROCCO

These are the native countries of the *Barb* or *Berber*, descended from the ancient *Numidian* horse. It has the same hardy constitution and docile temperament as the *Arab*, although the conformation is different, as the *Barb* has flat shoulders, a rounded chest, longer head and the tail is set comparatively low—a feature which may be observed in other breeds of horses which have *Barb* blood.

There are said to be several different strains, 'the first of which was reared by the Mograbins on the western side of the plains south of the Atlas, to whom it was known as "Shrubat-ur-rich"—Drinker of the Wind. These horses were either grey or brown in colour, low and greyhound like in shape and carried very little flesh. More remarkable is the *Bornu* breed, from the district south of Lake Chad, which is greyish white in colour with black legs. The tail is set rather low, the legs and feet are beautifully made and the body is relatively short. A third breed occurs typically in the Dongola district of Nubia, but is also found in Alfaia and Gerri'.* The latter types were smaller. Other types are given by General Daumas: *Haymour*, generally brown; *Ben Ghareb*, grey, not very fast but very enduring; and the *Merizig*, which is small and hardy.

When we remember that the Muslim invasions of Spain brought both *Arab* and *Barb* horses into the country, it is not surprising that the characteristic colouring of some horses in the peninsula is grey with black points. Furthermore, grey or dun horses with black points are characteristic of many horses of South America. It seems possible that the word *Barb* designated the horses ridden by barbarian invaders!

Obviously the *Barb* of today has some *Arab* blood. These horses are particularly valued as remounts for the French Spahis, who were part of the Turkish cavalry prior to 1836. The most important stud is at Constantine, where great efforts are made to keep the *Barb* to its ancient form.

There are many qualities in this breed which add up to a really good saddle horse. Unfortunately, it is almost unknown outside its own countries, but as the influence of *Barb* blood was proved in Spain a thousand years ago and later in South America, it would surely be of value if more interest could be taken. (See pp. 196-197).

CAMEROON REPUBLIC

Fulani tribesmen in the French Cameroon Republic have produced a breed of horses again very similar to the *Basuto* pony. The Fulanis are a nomadic tribe who originated

*R. S. Summerhays: *Observer's Book of Horses and Ponies.*

in the Upper Nile Valley and worked their way south. These horses have been used for many years by British troops as pack ponies and for reconnaissance. (See p. 198).

NIGERIA

Nigeria has two types of native horses—large and small. No particular care appears to be used in breeding these animals, which surely have a mixture of *Barb* blood. (See pp. 199).

BASUTOLAND

In South Africa the best known local breed is the *Basuto* pony, which is a cross between *Arab*, *Persian*, and *Thoroughbred* and is bigger than the primitive ponies of other parts of the continent. The *Basuto* pony makes a good pack and saddle horse. The breed appeared first about the middle of the 17th century, brought by the Dutch and Portuguese to the Cape and it was then called the *Cape Horse*. These horses gained a high reputation during the Boer War.

Basutoland acquired the *Cape Horse* as a result of Zulu raids about 1822. As these horses were continually ridden at fast speeds over rocky ground up and down hills, they have become quite fearless and sure-footed and have amazing stamina. The *Basuto* pony is used in South Africa for racing and polo. (See p. 200).

MADAGASCAR

This is one of the largest islands in the world and has a native pony breed called the *Madagascan* pony.

ETHIOPIA AND ERITREA

These countries have the *Dongola* horse. This breed is a mixture of *Barb* and other Oriental breeds. The horses are used for racing in Addis Ababa and a number are bred in private studs by the Negus.

In the second century A.D., the present countries of Ethiopia and Somaliland were known as Barbary; later almost the whole portion of North Africa was generally called Barbary. Some 2,000 years earlier the Nubians and Libyans had fused as a race of people; the Sahara cave paintings on the Tassili-Ahaggar Plâteau are dated around 1200 B.C. These show horses and chariots and mounted horsemen. Perhaps it is to this period that we could look for the origin of *Barb* horses, although, as I have suggested elsewhere, the name may also have been bestowed on the horses of 'barbarian' invaders. During the zenith of Greek power almost anyone who was not Greek was a barbarian!

194

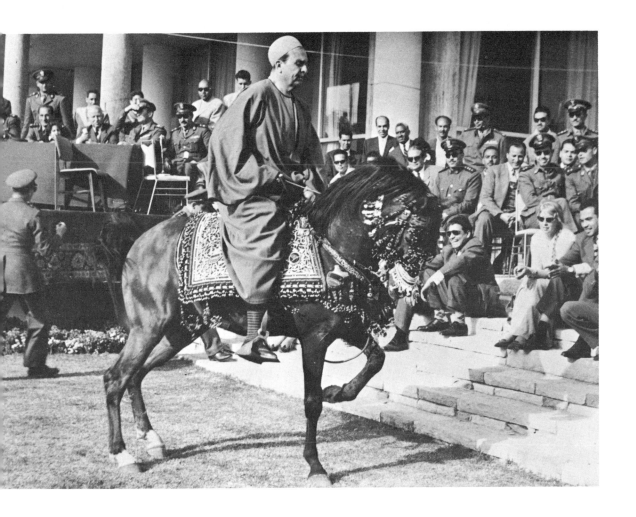

Egyptian
Arab

Locality: Egypt–Studs at El Zahraa and Ein Shams.

Colour and characteristics: Often grey, but other colours. Bred for racing. Pure-bred desert horses of both *Kuhaylan* and *Siglavy* types. The *Kuhaylan* is of rangier conformation, with excellent shoulders; quarters (by comparison with the *Siglavy*) long; erect neck and straight head; rather longer ears. The *Siglavy* has a compact, well-rounded body; good, clean legs; beautiful, concave face, small head and ears; large, lively eye, stallions bold eye; mares soft.

Height: Varies: About 14·2 to 14·3 h.h. $7\frac{1}{2}$-$7\frac{3}{4}$ inches bone.

There are two first-class Arabian studs, El Zahraa and Ein Shams, where pure-bred *Arabs* are bred and exported to many countries. 'Dancing' horses were first heard of in Persia many centuries B.C. *Arabs,* performing at the Feast of Luxor, must be sensitive to the aids and to music and require very careful training.

195

Libyan Barb

Locality: North Africa, Libya.
(*See* Barb, Algeria).

The *Libyan Barb*—or perhaps more justifiably the 'North African horse', because it is really descended from two breeds, the pure-bred *Arab* and the *Barb*—is used by tribesmen, civilians and the armed forces all along the north coast of Africa. It has a good constitution and is also very active though not particularly beautiful. Its conformation is not as regular as it might be, because outside blood, brought in by the many invasions and migrations, has been added in addition to the two breeds mentioned above.

Barb

Locality: North Africa – Algeria, Morocco.

Colour and characteristics: Generally dark bay, brown, chestnut, black and grey. Characteristically flat shoulders, sloping quarters, with low-set tail; head concave.

Height: 14 to 15 h.h.

The native home of the *Barb* is Algeria—where there is a large stud in Constantine —and Morocco. There were several strains varying a little one from the other. From about 800 A.D. Oriental horses including *Barbs* were imported in great numbers into Spain, considerably influencing the *Andalusian* and *Spanish* horse, and through them most of the other breeds of horses in Europe. Today the *Barb* possesses a certain amount of *Arab* blood, although attention is paid to keeping the type to the ancient *Barb*. It is extraordinarily hard, docile, and can live on small quantities of poor fare. It has a relatively long head, flat shoulders and the tail is set fairly low. It is essentially a riding horse and of an older breed than the *Arab*; it therefore seems a pity that breeding is confined almost exclusively to the north coast of Africa.

197

Fulani
Horse

Locality: Cameroon Republic.

Colour and characteristics: All colours. In conformation very mixed.

Height: About 14 h.h.

Horses bred by the nomadic Fulani tribesmen near Bamenda, on the borders of the Cameroons and Nigeria, are small, tough and hardy, but are a very mixed breed with some Oriental blood. They are used as pack and saddle horses.

198

Nigerian Horse

Locality: Nigeria.

Colour and characteristics:
All colours. Conformation
varies; generally rather
plain head; unremarkable
neck on good shoulders;
quarters inclined to be
weak; hard legs and feet.
A hardy, willing
unobtrusive pony.

Height: About 14 to
14·2 h.h.

Very little is known of any particular breed of Nigerian horse. These horses clearly show *Barb* influence and very probably horses were brought into Nigeria in the same way that they came to other parts of Africa—via imports or nomadic tribes.

Basuto Pony

Locality: Basutoland.

Colour and characteristics: Usually chestnut, bay, brown, grey; white markings allowed. Small and thickset, with longish back; short legs and exceptionally hard hooves. This pony often shows quality.

Height: About 14·2 h.h.

There are quite a number of pony breeds in South Africa. One of the best known is the hardy *Basuto* pony, although like the others it is not indigenous to the country. It is mainly descended from the *Arab* and *Barb* horses imported from Java in 1653. These became the ancestors of the *Cape* horse (which is said to have influenced the Australian *Waler*—see p. 205) and was the direct ancestor of the *Basuto* pony.

200

AUSTRALASIA

AUSTRALIA. Brumby; Waler.

NEW ZEALAND. Native Pony.

AUSTRALASIA

AUSTRALIA

Australia is said to be one of the oldest existing land masses and consists of a vast plâteau, bounded on the east by the Great Dividing range and elsewhere by low sandy shores. To the west lies the Indian Ocean, to the north the Indonesian islands and New Guinea, on the east the Pacific Ocean with New Zealand.

Although the aborigines, possibly coming originally from the Malay Peninsula, have proved themselves excellent horsemen and stockmen, they found no horses in Australia nor do they appear to have brought any with them. The entire horse population of Australia has been imported since its discovery by Spanish and Portuguese explorers in the 16th century. About a hundred years later trading ships from the Cape of Good Hope touched the west and north-west shores and possibly the first horses to land were the *Cape Horses* (See *Basuto* pony, p. 200).

Later there followed imports of many different breeds, including naturally the *Thoroughbred*. Eventually, horse-breeding became a serious business.

The horses of western Australia are descendants of Indonesian ponies (see pp. 176-181) and are small in size. The *Waler* is a mixture of many breeds and gets his name from the State of New South Wales, which together with Queensland and Victoria proved climatically ideal for breeding superior saddle horses and remarkable jumpers. These horses are much in demand and were exported to India as remounts, artillery horses and race horses. In 1940 the world high jump record of 8ft. 4ins. was made by an Australian *Waler*.

During the gold rush of 1851, horse breeding was sadly neglected and the animals strayed, breeding indiscriminately on the ranges. Inferior scrub horses, known as *Brumbies*, were the result and in time they became completely wild. Unfortunately these horses are generally considered to be useless when broken-in—or it may be the method of breaking them that makes them useless. *Brumbies* had so increased in 1962 to the west of Brisbane that mechanised efforts were being made to catch them and turn them into profit in the shape of cat's meat.

Australia has *Arab*, *Thoroughbred* and *Trotter* studs. The *Arabian* breed is increasing and half-bred *Arabs* are highly valued. The biggest private studs are the Fenwick Arab Stud (Melbourne), the Newbridge Stud (Sydney) and the Stony Park East Stud (Albury). (See pp. 204-205).

NEW ZEALAND

The first importations of horses into New Zealand took place around 1773 and conditions are ideal for breeding. Horses are used for stock-keeping and for various sports. Both Australia and New Zealand breed and race *Thoroughbreds. Arabs* from India were first imported in 1922 and later from the Wentworth stud at Crabbet Park, England. In New Zealand the *Arabian* studs of Woodstock and Ngairoiti are well-known. New Zealand claims the world's fastest pacer in the seven-year-old Cardigan Boy, winner of the Inter-Dominion Championship and the New Zealand Cup. On December 22nd, 1963, he ran $1\frac{5}{8}$ miles in 3·18, 1/5—about 1·56,3/5 to the mile. The American Adios Butler's time is 1·54,3/5. But New Zealand has claimed that Cardigan Boy can go 1·54,1/5 against time. (See p. 206).

Locality: Australia – Mainly west of Brisbane, Queensland.

Colour and characteristics: All colours. Generally degenerated ('scrub') horses descended from domestic species gone wild; almost impossible to tame.

Height: Varies considerably.

Brumby

In the early days, a number of horses wandered off from the settlers' encampments into the wild scrub country. When caught some prove to be excellent, but on the whole they are said to be useless on account of their wild natures. *Brumbies*, as they were called, had increased so much by 1962 that about 8,000 were estimated to be roaming 700 miles west of Brisbane, and hunters with light planes and jeeps set out to catch them. A local stock agent said that the horses were a lot smarter than the hunters believed, as they knew every inch of the timbered, stony country, and men who had lived in the area for years had not been able to catch them.

Waler

Locality: Australia – New South Wales.

Colour and characteristics: All colours. Type varies. Good shoulder, strong back and quarters, and particularly good hocks.
Often possessing great jumping ability.

Height: Varies. Generally desired about 16 h.h.

This photograph shows a typical Australian *Waler* used by the New South Wales Mounted Police. Bred within 40 years of the first settlement in Australia, *Walers*—so named after the original colony of New South Wales—had a reputation for soundness and endurance and were much in demand as cavalry remounts. During the first World War more than 120,000 Australian horses were exported for the allied armies in India, Africa, Palestine and Europe. With a diminishing demand for *Walers*, horse breeders now concentrate on the lighter bloodstock types.

205

Native Pony

Locality: New Zealand – Not limited.

Colour and characteristics: Any colour and of variable conformation.

Height: Around 14·2 h.h.

The New Zealand cow pony is very often cross-bred. Much of New Zealand's original stock came from Australia and found very favourable climatic conditions. There are several good types of pony and light horse; and a number of studs for *Thoroughbreds* and *Trotters*.

206

NORTH AMERICA

UNITED STATES. American Thoroughbred; Quarter Horse; American Saddle Horse (Kentucky Saddler); Tennessee Walking Horse; Missouri Fox-Trotting Horse; Morgan; Standardbred Trotter; Spanish Mustang; 'Wild Horses' of Wyoming; Galiceño; Chincoteague and Assateague Ponies; American Cleveland Bay; American Hackney Pony; American Hackney Horse; American Welsh Pony; American Shetland Pony; Pony of the Americas; Pinto (Paint) Horse; Appaloosa; Palomino; Albino; American Percheron; American Belgian.

CANADA. Royal Canadian Mounted Police Horse; Sable Island Pony; Canadian Cutting Horse.

MEXICO. Native Mexican.

NORTH AMERICA

The continent of North America consists of two very large countries—Canada and the United States of America. Canada is bounded to the north by the Arctic Ocean and to the east by the Atlantic Ocean, which is also the eastern boundary of the U.S.A. To the south the United States are bounded by the Gulf of Mexico, Mexico and the Pacific Ocean, with the northern territory of Alaska to the north-west of Canada. The climate is one of wide differences of temperatures and rainfall. In those parts of both Canada and the United States where they are bred, the horses are subjected to temperatures similar to those of Europe and northern Asia.

In 1950 the census showed that there were 7,981,000 horses and mules in the U.S.A., but no figures are available for Canada.

An interesting fact is that the New World—as the Spanish discoverers of the 15th and 16th centuries called the continents of North and South America—is comparable to Australasia in that there are no indigenous breeds of horses or ponies. Some hundreds of thousands of years ago prehistoric *equus* roamed the vast plains; some are thought to have crossed the Bering Straits to Asia and Europe when climate and temperatures differed from those of the present day. For some unknown reason horses finally became extinct in the Americas.

The West Indies provides the link between the continents of North and South America, for it was to the island of Hispaniola, or Haiti, that Christopher Columbus first arrived in 1493 and brought with him thirty horses, of which ten were mares. This was a momentous occasion in the history of the horse in the western hemisphere. With every ship that subsequently set sail from Spain for the New World a number of horses were included.

From the time of the Moslem conquest in the 8th century, Spain had been inundated with *Barb* horses from Morocco and Algeria. The *Barb* stallion, Guzman, founded a breed *Guzmanes* on the original native Spanish horses. From these crossed with *Arabian* blood sprang the *Andalusian,* bred in the province of Andalusia. (See p. 262). Seven hundred years later representatives of this breed, together with fresh additions of *Barb* blood, founded the first studs on Hispaniola and by 1500 the Spanish had at least one ranch with sixty brood mares.

When one considers that the voyage from Cadiz took about three months, that the horses stood tied on the open deck of these sailing ships, in wind and storm, with no cover and no exercise and that losses were often as much as fifty per-cent, the speed with which the horse population increased in the New World is truly amazing. Before a hundred years had passed there were horses on all the islands and the mainland and at least four different types—parade horses, racehorses, war horses and those used for pack and transport.

The photograph on p. 263 shows the ponies of Haiti and it seems more than likely that these are the most immediate descendants of those horses brought by Columbus and the Conquistadores who followed him.

Diego de Velasquez conquered Cuba with only eight horses and mares and from there Hernán Cortés, a wealthy stockman and rancher, set forth to settle Mexico. Within a very short time on the plentiful grazing there were several provinces boasting of first-class horses. By the middle of the 16th century there was a tremendous boom in horses, increased by the opening of the silver mines and by the growth of cattle-ranching. By about the year 1600 new-comers to the lost province of Cinero found large numbers of livestock grazing along the river meadows, in all about 10,000. As Robert Moorman Denhardt says in *The Horse of the Americas:* 'A better illustration to explain the origin of the semi-feral mustangs and wild cattle could hardly be cited'.

Shiploads of Irish horses arrived in Virginia in 1620 and subsequently the Swedes, Finns and Dutch brought in their own breeds. The English brought up Spanish stock from the southern states and soon there were wild herds to be found on the borders of Virginia. Some of these small horses were crossed with imported English horses and thus founded the *Narragansett Pacer,* which became part ancestor of the *Quarter Horse* (see pp. 218-219).

THE UNITED STATES

The Spaniards brought horses to North America by four different routes—California, New Mexico, Texas and Florida. In a very short time the Indian tribes had acquired horses, usually by raids. They very soon proved themselves to be superb horsemen.

The rapid increase of the horse population by the end of the 17th century is fully appreciated when one realises that there were herds running wild from Mexico to the Canadian border. By the middle of the 19th century the half-wild *Mustang* had turned into the invaluable cow-pony and so eventually the *Quarter Horse* was bred. And with the breeding of the *Quarter Horse* by the early colonials there came into being all the activities for which horses of this breed can be used—racing, the rodeo and riding for pleasure.

This breed originated during the colonial era about three hundred years ago, when horses were raced about 440 yards and thus acquired the colloquial name 'quarter miler'. Their origin lies in the horses brought by the Spaniards which were then crossed with mares brought over from England early in the 17th century, and the breed became established at the beginning of the 19th century. The horse is regarded

209

as a hot-blood and is extremely prepotent; because of its excellent qualities the breed has spread far and wide across the States to Canada. There are now over 134,000 *Quarter Horse* registrations.

The *American Saddle Horse, or Kentucky Saddler,* is a stylish and effective parade horse. This breed was developed by Kentucky pioneers as a utility horse, with easy gaits and gentle temperament. It has substance, quality and stamina. The *Kentucky Saddler* is derived from several other breeds or types. In fact if the horse is carefully studied there is more resemblance to the *Hackney;* and like the *Hackney* some *Saddlers* are brilliant show-jumpers; the breed is, however, most generally appreciated for its five gaits—trot, canter, rack, slow gait and walk.

The founder of the breed was Denmark and his son, Denmark 61, out of a pacing mare.

The *Tennessee Walking Horse* is regarded primarily as a show and pleasure horse and he is famous for his easy gaits. The breed was developed in Tennessee, about a hundred years ago, from the *Morgan, Narragansett Pacer* (Rhode Island), *Canadian Pacer,* the *American Saddle Horse* and the *Thoroughbred.* Allan F–1, Black Allan and his son, Roan Allan, founded the breed. Over 50,000 horses are registered.

The *Missouri Fox Trotter* is one of the oldest but least known breeds, dating back to 1820 when settlers came to the Ozark Hills of Missouri and Arkansas from Kentucky, Tennessee and Virginia. They brought *Thoroughbred, Arab* and *Morgan* horses with them. The mares were bred to the fastest sires and great families were developed, taking their names from the characteristics or the name of a great and potent sire. Often the owners believed that their animals were pure-bred and boasted that their horse was a pure-bred Brimmer, Colddeck, Copper Bottom, etc.

The Brimmers probably originated from a horse called Goode's Old Brimmer, and thus traced to the *Thoroughbred,* Imp. Jolly Roger. Moses Locke Alsup, belonging to a famous racing family, owned Old Brimmer, who was a potent sire and a great winner of races. Finally selective in-breeding took place and so a distinct type became fixed. As racing declined and was finally outlawed, the Brimmers and similar horses became the utility horse of the Ozarks. They were the principal means of transportation. They carried the young man courting and to social gatherings of all kinds; sometimes his lady rode behind him on the same horse. Occasionally she had her own *Fox Trotting* horse. My American correspondent vouches that either way was entirely satisfactory to court a girl over half a century ago—and he still has the lady as proof.

The *Missouri Fox Trotter* breed has been enhanced in recent years by additions of *American Saddle Horse* and *Tennessee Walking Horse* blood; but the typical broken gait, fore feet walking and hind feet trotting, remains.

The *Morgan* is an altogether different type and breed, used under the saddle and in harness. Descent is from Justin Morgan, foaled in 1790 in Massachusetts, who is thought to have been by the *Thoroughbred* True Briton, who was a very fertile sire. Mares of the following breeds were in the New England States at the time of Justin Morgan's conception: the Norwegian *Fjord*, the *Friesian* or *Harddraver* and the *Norfolk Trotter*. Although one prominent American writer ascribes Justin Morgan's origin on the female side to the *Fjord*, the author differs and considers that he probably had a considerable amount of *Norfolk Trotter* blood in his pedigree; the stamp, action and colour *even now* of the *Morgans* suggest a connection with the old *Norfolk Trotter*, which was also a prepotent harness/saddle horse. The world's champion pacing stallion, the celebrated Dan Patch (1896), had much Morgan blood in his pedigree.

Another great trotting breed is the American *Standardbred* (p. 226), which owed its origin to imported horses such as the *Thoroughbred,* Messenger, 'the father of the trotters', of whom it was said that, as he passed over the gangway of the ship that took him from England to America in 1788, it meant 20,000,000 sovereigns to the people of the United States; and to Bellfounder as well as many Dutch *Harddraver* horses. There are two important lines in the *Standardbred* family—Peter the Great, descended from Hambletonian 10, and Axworthy. The two stallion lines of the *Pacers* are Billy Direct and Abbedale. Some pacing stallions are also to be found in the first two stallion lines. When racing, horses must maintain their proper stride—e.g., if a trotting race, they must not change to pacing, and if pacing they are not allowed to break to a trot on pain of disqualification. There are no fewer than 873 trotting tracks in the United States.

The *Spanish Mustang* is descended from the horses which were turned loose when no longer needed by the Conquistadores. The descendants of these horses, known as *Mustangs*, migrated through Mexico to the United States, scattering far west and north-west. Some were captured by the Indians and subsequently became *Indian* ponies; others proved to be the foundation for many American breeds of horses; others again remained in ever smaller numbers (since the wholesale massacre that took place at the end of the last war, to feed European populations) in the wild state. There are only twenty-five or thirty registered mares and stallions.

A further number of breeds have been developed, having been imported from other countries. The most recent importation, in 1959 from Mexico, is the *Galiceño*; others include the *Shetland* pony which bears little resemblance to its ancestor from Northern Britain. In many ways this pony now looks like a miniature *Hackney*, with artificially developed gaits. The Society concerned claims that over 100,000 ponies are registered, 80 per cent of this number during the past twenty years. Seventy-five thousand ponies are reckoned to be living to-day.

The American Shetland Pony Club now has over 6,000 members, with members in all fifty states, and also in Canada. Apart from Harness and Racing contests, one of the newer fields is that of Pulling Contests, where ponies pull on a percentage of weight. One interesting note is that ponies can pull as much as 200 per cent on weight where the

211

best draught or work horses cannot pull more than their own weight. The world record stallion sold for the sum of 85,000 dollars in 1957.

The 'wild' *Chincoteague* and *Assateague* ponies are to be found on both these islands, off the coast of Virginia and Maryland. On Pony Penning Day, the last Thursday and Friday of July, ponies are rounded up and made to swim the channel dividing Assateague from Chincoteague (pronounced 'shin-ca-teeg') where the sales are held. The origin of these ponies is obscure, but they are probably descended from horses that either strayed or were abandoned in the early American colonial days. Their characteristics are rather those of stunted horses than ponies—the pony qualities are lacking. Many are paint or pinto colours (piebald and skewbald).

The *Arabian* breed (see Asia) is extremely popular in the United States for its great qualities of endurance. Height varies from 14 h.h. and has reached 16 h.h. and this may well become the normal height in the United States, owing to the 'growing methods' of the breeders. The reader is referred to remarks in the introduction that stress conditions, climate, food. There are many studs for pure-bred *Arabs* including the Kellogg Institute at Pamona, California; the San Simeon Stables, Hearst Ranch, California; the Van Fleet Arabian Stud near Denver, Colorado; Paenonian Springs, Virginia; Jordan Arabian Farm, New York; Al-Marah Arabian Farm, Washington D.C., and the Joder Arabian Farm also in Colorado.

The *Cleveland Bay* horse was first imported from Great Britain in 1820 and the Cleveland Bay Society of America was founded in 1885. 1,280 stallions and over 500 mares were registered in the Stud Book, before it was closed, although some *Cleveland Bay* horses have been imported in recent years. The breed is very prepotent and produces an excellent medium and heavy hunter when crossed with the *Thoroughbred*. Breeders also cross them with small range mares to produce good solid cow horses.

The *Icelandic* pony and the *Welsh* pony are further importations. The latter makes an ideal children's riding pony, especially for jumping, and harness pony. Small *Hackneys* or *Bantam Hackneys* were established by breeding to *Welsh* ponies, *Arabs* and, in Britain, to the *Fell* pony; but the Registry does not distinguish between a *horse* and *pony*. The *Connemara* pony also has its own Registry.

The type called *Pony of the Americas* was founded only ten years ago and therefore may scarcely be termed a breed. A well-known American writer and judge defined a breed: 'A number of animals which possess certain common and well-defined characteristics that distinguish them from others of the species, and which are so endowed as to consistently transmit such distinguishing characteristics to their progeny', to which the author added: 'And which characteristics have been transmitted over at least ten generations'. The distinguished American replied: 'You have more time to do things than we have'.

The *Pony of the Americas,* however, does describe itself as a breed—a western type utility pony, with *Appaloosa* colour and characteristics.

212

Many societies in America specialise in encouraging colour, such as the *Pinto* or *Painted Horse*, whose association was formed in 1956. Many 'paints' are *Quarterbred*. Another colour is that of the *Appaloosa* or *Palouse* horse, originally bred by the Nez Percé Indians (see p. 242). 'Today there are several strains of colour which are being selectively bred. They include *Palomino, Appaloosa, Pinto*, leopard-spotted *Colorado Rangers, Albino*, zebra-duns and grullos. Perhaps the most striking coat to appear on a horse is that of the *Appaloosa*, the beautiful horse with the spotted rump. Horses of this sort are also known by the colour name: blanket, polka dot, raindrop, leopard-spot, dollar-spot, harlequin, spotted-rump, speckled tails, etc'.*

The word pinto is derived from the Spanish word *'pintado',* meaning painted. The cowboys used it as a collective term to denote spotted horses in general, but also as a specific term to indicate the *Tobiano* type of coloured horse. The term 'paint horse' is the result of the Indian's penchant towards painting designs on the white patches on his horse. Most two-colour Indian ponies were *Overos,* hence 'overo' and 'paint' became synonymous. The *Morocco* type is the third colour pattern. In Europe the colour is more generally known as piebald or skewbald (black and white and white and any colour except black); the colour is found in different breeds of horses and ponies in many countries across the world, including Australia with their *Pinto Standardbred Trotter.*

Palomino is a popular colour both in the western and eastern hemisphere. It is thought to have originated in Spain under the name Ysabella or Isabella, after the Spanish queen (1451-1504) who did so much to encourage exploration of the New World. Undoubtedly it is due to Spanish blood that the *Palomino* colour arrived in the Americas. *Palomino* is no special breed, for Texas likes the *Quarter Horse* type, Colorado the *Thoroughbred,* California the *Arab,* while other states prefer the *American Saddle Horse* type.

Palomino does not necessarily beget *Palomino* and many other colours may appear; it is almost impossible to establish a breed on a colour, for although a colour may subsequently be a characteristic of a breed with many other characteristics, colour by itself does not indicate a breed. If the horse (or pony) can be standardised then perhaps at some time in the future it may establish itself as a breed.

The *Colorado Ranger* traces its origins back to two stallions, a *Barb* and an *Arab* presented to General Grant, President of the United States, by the Sultan of Turkey. Then a *Moroccan Barb* was imported and the offspring were crossed with a *Barb* leopard from Andalusia. Although the *Ranger* and the *Palouse* often have coats of a similar colour, the former are said not to be related to the Indian ponies. A characteristic of the *Ranger* is the flowing mane and tail.

The American *Albinos* are foaled pure white with a pink skin and trace their ancestry back to Old King, a pure-white stallion foaled in 1906. Old King had a

*Denhardt: *The Horse of the Americas.*

213

spotless pink skin, milky-white coat with a long silky mane and tail and dark brown eyes. The Secretary of the White Horse Ranch, Nebraska, stresses that modern *Albinos* do not have pink eyes. *Albinos* are of *Morgan-Arabian* descent. There are four classifications for *Albino* breeding. The colour is becoming extremely popular throughout Nebraska and other parts of the U.S.A.

Dun and grullo (crane) coloured horses are thought to have exceptional stamina, the belief also being held in South America and Europe. The horses are known as 'coyote dun' or 'zebra dun' and the latter, like the mouse-coloured grullo, has black points, black dorsal stripe and usually stripes on the legs. Some grullos vary from a pale salt-and-pepper to blue and mauve. These colours incidentally, when not mixed with white hairs, are common to some Eastern European ponies, especially those which are fairly nearly descended from the *Tarpan* (see p. 39).

Once again we can trace the Western horse, through his Oriental forebears, back to the prehistoric horses of the steppes of Asia and the plains and forests of Europe. And since he may have begun his travels hundreds of thousands of years ago by going westward to Asia and Europe *from* the North American continent, he has thus completed the full circle and is today to be found on the Texas plains with the same colour coat as his prehistoric ancestors.

America imported the first *Thoroughbred*, a horse called Bull Rock, from England in 1730, and was one of the first countries to recognise the real value of this breed; after England, America was the first country to breed them. Today Virginia and Kentucky rival one another in breeding and racing.

The first *Percherons* shipped to America arrived in 1839. The Percheron Society of America, now called the Percheron Horse Association of America, was established in 1905. This was the first heavy breed to be imported and *Percherons* are the most numerous in the United States and in Canada.

The breed expanded well until the nineties, when depression struck the country. No further horses were imported, and large breeding herds were dispersed; good horses were therefore distributed over a larger area. By 1910, 31,900 horses were registered.

Belgian horses have been imported for some years. The early horses were bay, but sorrels and roans are now increasing and also chestnuts, all with a tendency towards lighter manes and tails.

The greatest number of *Suffolk* horses are registered in the eastern states; they are noted for a long life and fertility, and stallions have been used to improve other draught horses or to breed heavy-weight hunters from *Thoroughbred* mares. For the history of the *Shire* and the *Clydesdale,* see under Great Britain. *Percheron, Belgian* and *Shire* are the most popular breeds. Colours are bay, brown, black, chestnut, grey and roan. The latter colour is rarely seen in Great Britain today.

The American Cream Draft Horse Association is the first heavy horse breed to base its requirements on colour. It was founded in 1944, on a *Cream* foundation mare

214

called Old Granny; her son, Nelson's Buck 2, is regarded as the progenitor of the breed. Breeding continued by using other draught breeds including a *Percheron*, a *Shire* and a *Belgian* mare. The colour is cream with white mane and tail and a pink skin. Foals are born with nearly white eyes that begin to turn darker at one year and are a clear amber when full grown. Minimum weight is 1100 lbs. The *Costoñega* is the heaviest native American draught horse. (Canada also uses the *Clydesdale*, crossed with other types).

CANADA

The first horses were brought into Canada about 1665 by the French. The French, too, are supposed to have taken horses early in the 18th century to Sable Island, some two hundred miles out in the Atlantic off the coast of Nova Scotia. On this treeless windswept island, roughly twenty-five miles in length, there are about three hundred semi-wild scrub horses, descendants of the French horses.

They are divided into small herds of about six to eight mares with a stallion who fights valiantly against usurpers. The herds remain within their own locality and roam no further than a mile or so.* They live without shelter all the year, but the winters on Sable Island are not severe. During the winter they eat snow for water or break holes in the ice with their hooves. Many Nova Scotian farmers use *Sable Island* ponies. They are small, wiry and of good conformation; if caught young they can be broken easily. Their colour is grey, sorrel, black, brown and chestnut.

There are, of course, Canadian ranches which breed cow-ponies. But one of the most interesting breeding establishments was founded by the Royal Canadian Mounted Police in 1940 at Fort Walsh, consisting of some 15,000 acres. Until this time the Force had been dependent upon outside sources for its remounts. Although the number of remounts required has been lessened by the aeroplane and motorisation, the Force sticks to its belief in the value of equitation as a 'means of developing self-confidence, determination and respect for discipline and the challenge it offers to intellect, nerve and ability'.**

The remounts are of no particular breed, but as the photograph on p. 249 shows, a definite type appears to have been established by crossing *Thoroughbred* stallions on cold-blood or half-bred mares. Twenty-five black and dark brown mares are bred from every year and average eighteen foals. Horses must be black or dark brown. One black stallion and one brown are used for this purpose, but occasionally dark bay foals are born and they must be relegated to the riding school.

There are seventy horses each at the training centres at Regina and Ottawa used for training recruits, Ceremonial Parades and Musical Rides.

*The author was told that *Dartmoor* ponies in South-west England also keep to similar feeding areas.
**From a paper sent to the author by the Office of the Royal Canadian Mounted Police, Ottawa.

215

Canada has *Thoroughbred* and *Trotter* studs. The following breeds of ponies are recognised by the Canadian Pony Society, which was formed in 1901—*Shetland*: reg. to 1962 4,558. *Welsh*: 1,383. *Welsh F.S.*: 213. *Polo*: 7. *Dartmoor*: 46. *Highland*: 13. *Fell*: 18. *Exmoor*: 375. *Iceland*: 1,135. *New Forest*: 5.

Breeders have developed a 'modern' type of Shetland pony (see illustration under U.S.A.). This pony has more style, is more balanced in conformation, and has a flashy action both at the walk and trot.

The census taken in 1931 showed an equine population of 578,157 horses, of heavy, light and pony breeds, which are all imported as in the United States. In 1961 the number had decreased to 88,000. *Thoroughbreds* and *Standardbreds* have a great majority over all other breeds, which also include the *Canadian Hunter*, *Arab* and *Anglo-Arab*, *American Saddle*, *Quarter Horse*, *Palomino*, *Appaloosa* and *Tennessee Walking Horse*; the *Hackney*; and the *Belgian*, *Clydesdale* and *Percheron*.

On p. 251 may be seen a typical example of the Canadian Cutting Horse; this is not a separate breed, of course, but is a type of horse developed for rounding up cattle. There is a Canadian Cutting Horse Association.

American Thoroughbred

Locality: U.S.A. (*See* Great Britain).

Although Great Britain must rightly claim pride of place as the home of the *Thoroughbred*, other countries have not been slow in establishing the breed, so that it has really become international. Breeders in the United States have always bought first-class stock. A typical representative is Never Say Die, bred in America, a great winner on the flat. In 1962 Never Say Die headed the list of winning sires, his progeny earning £65,902. He won the St. Leger and the Derby, as did his son Larkspur. His sire Nasrullah was bred in England, and Never Say Die has raced only in England, where he now stands at the National Stud, West Grinstead.

217

Locality: U.S.A.

Colour and characteristics:
All solid colours (Paints
and Pintos not allowed).
Short, broad head; prick ears;
wide-set, kind eyes; sensitive
nostrils; strong jaws;
medium length, full, slightly
arched neck blends into
strong, sloping shoulders;
good whithers; closely-
coupled powerful back; broad,
deep and heavy quarters;
hocks wide, deep and straight;
flat, clean hard bone; strong
open feet. Active, balanced
horse, free from any sign
of nervousness.

Height: 15·2 to 16·1 h.h.

Quarter Horse

The *Quarter Horse* is considered to be both the oldest and the youngest breed of horses
in America. It originated during the colonial era in the Carolinas and Virginia, more
than 300 years ago. Match-racing was the leading sport, over a distance of about
440 yards, hence the colloquial name, 'quarter miler'—*Quarter Horse*. He is an
extraordinarily versatile animal, possessing inherent 'cow sense', and is used for racing
over short distances, for all rodeo contests—cutting, roping, barrel racing, bulldogging,
etc. It is claimed for the breed that they can do more jobs better than any other horse
in the world!

In American sports and show business there is nothing quite like a rodeo. It takes a
man to rope calves, wrestle steers, milk wild cows and ride broncos that do not wish to
be ridden. In recent years indeed rodeos have begun to rival baseball as a favourite
spectator sport. Millions of people watch these sports annually.

218

Quarter Horses in action at a rodeo at Salinas, California.

American Saddle Horse (Kentucky Saddler)

The American *Saddle Horse*, or *Kentucky Saddler*, is an excellent utility horse, of great beauty, easy gaits, gentle, even temperament, and possessing quality, stamina and substance. The breed has been developed from the *Thoroughbred* and *Morgan* and from *Narragansett Pacers* and *Trotters* brought to Virginia and Carolina by the early pioneers. The *Saddle Horse* is the best exponent of the five gaits—trot, canter, rack, slow gait and walk.

Locality: U.S.A.–Studs in Indiana, Kansas, Iowa, Louisville, Ohio, etc.

Colour and characteristics: Bay, brown, black and chestnut with white markings; also grey. A square horse covering much ground, of quite extraordinary presence. Small, elegant head on well-muscled 'swan neck', set well into powerful shoulders; muscular, pliable legs and joints; full mane and tail, usually nicked and carried artificially high. Tremendous, showy action in all gaits. Very fine satin coat.

Height: 15 to 16 h.h.
Weight: 1,000 to 1,200 lbs.

220

A GREY ARAB. This lovely Arabian horse, Shazda, is owned by Mrs Alexander of Marlborough, Wilts. The ever popular Arab is found in many countries of the world and has had an influence on many other breeds, including the Thoroughbred. (*Photograph by the author*)

A GREY THOROUGHBRED. The Thoroughbred has become an international breed. This is Mr Hugh Haldin's Cinderella Man, a champion hack, ridden by Miss Ann Davy. Under the name of The Hittite, he was raced successfully on the flat. (*Photograph by John Nestle*)

Tennessee Walking Horse

Locality: Tennessee and many other States; exported to South America.

Colour and characteristics: Black, white, bay, chestnut, roan and sorrel. Small head with prick ears; head is set on long, powerful neck, laid in to the shoulders and withers; square barrel; strong quarters; straight hind legs, forelegs and feet; tail carried exaggeratedly high. Particular emphasis is placed upon their running walk and docile and gentle natures.

Height: 15 to 15·2 h.h. **Weight:** 1,000 to 1,200 lbs.

The *Tennessee Walking Horse* is primarily what is called a 'show and pleasure horse', with quite extraordinarily pleasant and easy gaits, for which the horse is famous. There are roughly 4,000 registered animals, and it is said that the 'greatest tonic in the world is a ride on the back of a *Tennessee Walking Horse*'. The breed was developed in the Southern State as a mount for the cotton planter, from the *Plantation Ambler* later crossed with *Morgan, Narragansett Pacer, Canadian Pacer*, the *American Saddle Horse* and *Thoroughbreds*. Foremost founder of the breed was Allan F–1, Black Allan and his son, Roan Allan. The photograph shows the mare, Midnight Mystery, owned by Mr and Mrs John H. Amos (Franklin, Tennessee) and ridden by Winston Wiser.

223

Missouri Fox Trotting Horse

Locality: The Ozark Hills of Missouri and Arkansas.

Colour and characteristics: All colours from snow white to jet black; sorrels predominate and chestnut sorrels with white markings are general favourites. There are many *Palominos* represented in the breed, and where quality is evident *Pinto* and *Spotted* horses have been accepted. Compact, of good conformation and able to carry weight. Should stand well on its feet, be erect, wide awake and alert. The neck should be graceful in proportion to length of body, and well joined to the body; neat, clean, intelligently shaped head; pointed ears that are well shaped; large, bright eyes and a tapered muzzle; the back should be reasonably short and strong, the body deep and well ribbed.

Height: 14 to 16 h.h.

The 'fox trot' of the *Missouri Fox Trotting Horse* is a broken gait. It is a brisk walk with the fore feet and a trot with the hind feet. The tracks of the hind feet blot out or disfigure the tracks made by the fore. Many are five-gaited, but they show at the flat foot walk, fox trot and canter. When executing the fox trot the travelling horse nods his head with each step and his feet beat a rythmic sound on the trail as he travels. It is not a high stepping gait, but a sure-footed one; the horse travels at a speed of from five to ten miles an hour. *Below* Lucky Lad, owned by Hayden Evans, and *above* Prince Charming, owned by Mrs Joe R. Hinds–two champion *Missouri Fox Trotters*.

224

Morgan

Locality: U.S.A.

Colour and characteristics: Bay, chestnut, black and brown. Compact, muscular, solidly built horse; powerful shoulders; thick crested neck; well made legs and feet; full mane and tail. Very active.

Height: About 15·2 h.h. **Weight:** 800 to 1,000 lbs.

The *Morgan* horse is one of the few breeds to have derived its title from the name of the stallion who founded it—Justin Morgan, who was foaled about 1790 and owned by Thomas J. Morgan. Justin Morgan proved to be quite extraordinarily prepotent, although he was only by chance put to stud before being gelded. Not much is known of Justin Morgan's origin except that the *Thoroughbred*, True Briton (a descendant of the Byerley Turk), and a Dutch stallion claim the honour of siring him. However, the *Morgan* horse today is pure-bred and is used for riding or driving. They have influenced the breeding of the *Standardbred*, the *Saddle Horse* and the *Tennessee Walking Horse. Above* is Thirlstone Tip.

Standardbred Trotter

Locality: U.S.A. (dating from 1879).

Colour and characteristics: Any colour; usually chestnut, dun, black
and brown. Robust, muscular horse of slightly elongated conformation;
a *Thoroughbred* type, but with shorter legs and greater endurance;
very strong, hard shoulders and quarters; iron legs and good feet;
great action either as pacer or trotter.

Height: Average 15·2 h.h. **Weight:** 820 to 1,180 lbs.

The *Standardbred* is the official name for both pacers and trotters. Harness racing is
a most popular sport and the horses are bred with the greatest care. The breed goes
back to Hambletonian 10, foaled in 1849 and descended from Messenger, who was
imported in 1788, and Bellfounder, a *Norfolk Trotter,* who was imported in 1822.
The events leading to Hambletonian's birth are extraordinary. He left 1,321 foals.
The *Standardbred* is rather smaller than English-bred trotters or pacers; although
the chief breeding district is Kentucky, breeding is spread all over the United States
and Canada. There are 873 trotting tracks in the U.S.A.

Greyhound holds the world trotting record, made in 1938—1 mile in 1 min. 55¼ secs.
The pacers, Billy Direct and Adios Harry, did the same distance in 1 min. 55 secs.—
just a quarter of a second faster! The photograph *(opposite)* shows another famous
pacer, Adios Butler.

226

Standardbred pacers in action.

The famous pacer, Adios Butler.

Spanish Mustang

Locality: Mexico, California, and along the
Pacific coast, Idaho and Utah.

Colour and characteristics: Most colours, many
unusual, such as *grullo* (blue-grey crane colour
with black points mane and tail and list):
buckskin (dun, black points, mane and tail and
list); *navajo* (light background with 'red' splashes
– *navajo* means 'razor cut'). They are strong,
very hard horses, not particularly beautiful,
but extremely enduring.

Height: 14·2 to 15 h.h.

Three *Spanish Mustang* mares – Cedro, a true buckskin (dun) aged 24 years; Queenie,
a Crow Sundance Medicine Hat mare, aged 28 years, and Teton, a purple roan mare
aged 25 years. These are foundation *Spanish Mustang* mares, whose Registry was
formed in 1957 by Mr Robert Brislawn, who is the President. *Below* is a *Medicine
Hat* stallion, San Domingo. The *Medicine Hat* is a colour phase of the *Spanish
Mustang*.

228

'Wild' Horses of Wyoming

Locality: U.S.A. – Desert country of Wyoming.

Colour and characteristics: All colours, including the prominent *palomino*.
Mixed blood of Arab and many other breeds.

Height: Usually betweem 15 and 16 h.h.

In the red desert of Wyoming are to be found, just as in Australia, herds of 'wild' horses. But just as all horses in America are descended from the Spanish horses brought there by Cortés, and by subsequent importations in colonial days and later, these 'wild' horses are domesticated horses which over the years have reverted to nature. They were originally of *Arab, Barb, Turk, Cordovan* and other breeds. There are annual round-ups, and many horses in America owe their origin at least partly to these 'wild' horses—*Pinto* or *Paint Horses,* the *Indian Horse,* the *Palomino,* etc., which are not breeds but colours.

229

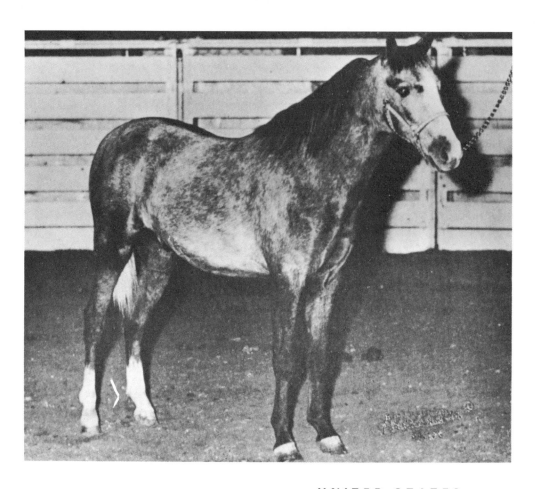

Galiceño

Locality: Coastal areas of Mexico and throughout the United States.

Colour and characteristics: Bay, black, sorrel and dun. A small horse
of compact build, looking rather 'fine'; shoulders inclined to be straight
with shallow chest; head shows character, with intelligent eyes;
feet are good and open at the heel. Natural running walk is very fast.

Height: 12 to 13·2 h.h.

Weight: 625 to 700 lbs.

The *Galiceño* breed was first imported into the United States in 1959 from Mexico,
where they are used for everyday transport and ranch work. It is thought that the
ancestors of these small horses may have been numbered among those that the
Spaniards originally brought to the New World via Hispaniola; and that these
ancestors were the *Garrano* or *Minho* ponies of Spain and Portugal. In the States,
and particularly in Texas, the *Galiceño* breed is found to be the ideal 'in-between'
mount. The *Galiceño* shown here is Gray Badger, winner at Fort Worth, Texas, shows.

230

UNITED STATES

Chincoteague and Assateague Ponies

Locality: Islands off the coast of Virginia and Maryland.

Colour and characteristics: Many are odd-coloured. Characteristics are those of stunted horses; they do not have 'pony' heads.

Height: Average 12 h.h.

These ponies are said to have inhabited the islands of Chincoteague ('Beautiful Land across the Waters') and Assateague, off the Virginian coast, since early colonial times. Assateague is uninhabited and consists of marsh, wood and meadowlands. On the last Thursday and Friday in July, the ponies–or rather small horses–on Assateague are collected and swim across the channel to Chincoteague, where they are sold by auction. The Assateague ponies are shown swimming and the Chincoteague ponies are collected for sale. (*Photographs by Virginia Department of Conservation and Economic Development*).

American Cleveland Bay

Locality: Mainly small numbers, in Virginia, Montana, Idaho and some other States.

Colour and characteristics: Always a whole bay colour with black points, mane and tail and black list; short, clean legs; action straight and true; high action not essential, but knees must flex.

Height: 15·2 to 16 h.h.

This *Cleveland Bay* stallion was bred in England by Captain L. Edmunds, of Salisbury, and imported and owned by Mr A. Mackay-Smith, President of the Cleveland Bay Society of America. Breeding of these good all-round horses is unfortunately on the decline; they have been driven off the land by the tractor, and hunter breeders prefer to breed the *Thoroughbred*, for which higher prices are obtainable. It should not be overlooked that the *Cleveland Bay* has the same mutual ancestors as the *Thoroughbred*. It is a breed of considerable stamina and energy.

American Hackney Pony

Locality: Throughout the United States and Canada.

Colour and characteristics: As for the *Hackney* horse. The American Hackney Horse Society Stud book does not distinguish between horse and pony; although small *Hackneys* should have defined pony characteristics and they are referred to as *Hackney Ponies* or *Bantam Hackneys*. Some breeds of small horses are not ponies, as they possess the characteristics of the horse and not those of the pony.

Height: 11 to 14·2 h.h. **Weight:** 650 to 850 lbs.

Red Letter is by King's Banner and is owned by Mr and Mrs F. L. Van Lennep of Michigan. This *Hackney Pony* is very attractive and full of action and fire, both essential qualities in a first-class harness horse or pony. Principal uses in the United States for *Hackneys* are: Showing in heavy harness, single, double team (pair) tandem, four-in-hand. Under the saddle; jumping, pleasure riding and some harness riding.

233

American Hackney Horse

Locality: Throughout the United States and Canada.

Colour and characteristics: Bay, black, brown, chestnut, roan and sorrel. For conformation see *Hackneys*, Great Britain, where this breed originated. The current fashion of tail nicking is greatly to be deplored; docking is a shorter and less painful operation.

Height: 14·2 to 16 h.h. and over.

Weight: 900 to 1,200 lbs.

Hackney Horses, through the *Norfolk Roadster*, have a pedigree going back even further than the *Thoroughbred*, from whom they are also descended; and through the *Thoroughbred* they also have *Arabian* and Oriental blood in their pedigrees. Two of the best known stallions in the United States are Cassilis Masterpiece and King's Banner. This charming pair, Cassilis Symphony and Stonhedge Danseuse, are driven by Mrs J. Macy Willets.

234

American Welsh Pony

In the United States the interest in *Welsh* ponies has grown so much that the number of registrations has increased tremendously and there are now a number of studs. Some of the best known studs in Wales have supplied new blood, so that the prospective breeder now has a generous assortment of ponies to choose from, when starting his own herd. The pictures show a stallion, Liseter Shooting Star, and a mare, Liseter Starlight, owned by Mrs J. A. du Pont.

Locality: Throughout the United States and Canada.

Colour and characteristics: The *Welsh Mountain Pony* and *Welsh Pony* refer to the same animal. All colours except odd colours (pinto). As children's riding ponies and show riding ponies for the smaller classes these ponies are unsurpassed, and they have few equals where small, light-hearted and courageous harness ponies are required for private use.

Height: The American Stud book limits the height to 12·2 h.h. (50 inches) at the withers. Ponies exceeding this height, but not exceeding 14 h.h., are listed by both British and American Stud books in Section 'B'.

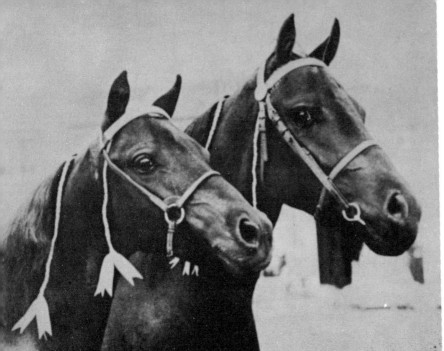

American Shetland Pony

Locality: Throughout the United States.

Colour and characteristics: All colours. They have proved to be profitable to raise. The breed is known for its hardiness and gentleness, and exhibits high intelligence. They are great companions for the entire family.

Height: Up to 46 inches.

Weight: Average 300 lbs.

Shetland Ponies are very diversified. They are shown throughout the United States in Halter Classes and Fine Harness Classes, where they are hitched to four-wheel buggies; they are also shown as Roadsters, hitched to two-wheeled carts. *Shetlands* are being raced in trotting races throughout the country today, and have some very fine records of 1:55 and less, on a one-half mile track. It does seem a pity, however, that in certain classes, the ponies are fitted with false hooves, to give them longer feet; that their tails are nicked and false tails are also added! There are three types – Riding type; Harness type; Draught Type. The pictures show registered American *Shetland* ponies.

UNITED STATES

Locality: Covers the United States and Canada.

Colour and characteristics: A Western type utility pony, conformation between *Arab* and *Quarter Horse* with *Appaloosa* colouring (see *Appaloosa*). The pony should show style, substance, beauty and symmetry.
Head shows character, with dished face accentuating Arabian characteristic; large, kind, prominent eyes; ears are pointed, alert and well-carried; body, round and full-ribbed; back and loins short, wide and well-muscled; good forearm; chest wide, deep and full; well-laid shoulders and withers; hindquarters long; level and muscular croup, quarters and gaskins. Good feet and legs; tail carried high. Action is that of a well-balanced riding pony. Six colour patterns.

Height: 11·2 to 13 h.h.

Pony of the Americas

The *Pony of the Americas* is a comparatively new type, founded some ten years ago, to supply a suitable pony for children up to sixteen years of age. There are twenty-four States and one Province (Canadian) P.O.A. Clubs. These ponies are required to have a definite type and standard and are used on trail rides. One pony, Apache Wampum, completed the 600 mile ride from Columbus Junction, Iowa, to Cheyenne, Wyoming, in 1961. Ponies are also raced and show jumped. Foundation sire, Black Hand, is shown here – and a children's race in progress.

Pinto
(Paint)
Horse

Locality: Throughout
the United States.

Colour and characteristics:
A general purpose riding
horse. The word 'pinto'
comes from the Spanish
word meaning 'painted' and
is used to describe two-
colour horses—called *Overo*
and *Tobiano*—similar to
those called in Europe
piebald or skewbald
(black-and-white or
white and any
other colour except black).

Height: Varies.

The Pinto Horse Association of America was established in 1956, in Ellington, Connecticut, and the *Pinto* was recognised as a breed in 1963. There is also an American Paint Stock Horse Association, with headquarters in Amarillo, Texas. The terms pinto and paint cover a wide variety of two-colour horses. The *Overo* stallion *(above)* is Buzz Bomb (owned by C. E. Herring). *Tobiano* is considered a 'dominant gene' and predominates in North America and Europe. *Overo* is considered a 'recessive gene' and predominates in South America and Asia.

238

A PALOMINO STALLION. In the United States the Palomino is increasingly popular. This is Kingsettle Zecchino, a famous stallion whose sire was imported from Wyoming by his owner, Mrs. Peter Howell, for her stud at Cholderton, near Salisbury, Wiltshire. (*Photograph by P. Russell Howell*)

THE LLANERO (PRAIRIE) HORSE. This typical Venezuelan Indian horse is owned by Mrs de Fries. The Llanero is often this dun colour, with dark mane and tail, although it can be of several other colours. (*Photograph by Mrs de Fries*)

240

Tobiano stallion, Magnifique, owned by Joan Borgstide.

Tobiano mare, Lady Buck, owned by Sandy Boone.

This *Overo* mare is Indian Lady, owned by Carolyn Dykes Hall.

Appaloosa

Locality: Today there are more of these horses in the West than in any other areas of the United States, although they are becoming popular in Texas, the South-West, Middle West and North-East. Over 4,000 horses are registered with the Appaloosa Horse Club.

Colour and characteristics: Coat patterns are: frost, leopard, marble, snowflake, blanket, white blanket; males tend towards more brilliant colouring than the females; sparse manes and tails, referred to as finger-tailed or rat-tailed. Conformation and soundness of great importance. Their uses are listed primarily as stock horse and pleasure horse.

Height: Not under 14 h.h.

Weight: 950 to 1,275 lbs.

There are many variations and combinations of coat patterns in the *Appaloosa* horse; but actually six basic and one marginal pattern in those registered, since not all spotted horses are genuine *Appaloosas*. The eye is encircled by white sclera; parti-coloured skin, and parti-coloured hoofs. Horses of this unusual colouring are represented in early Chinese art; and also in the much earlier Cave art at Pêche Merle. Like all other breeds of horses in the United States, they owe their appearance on this continent to Spanish importations in the Middle Ages. The large area of fertile land drained by the Palouse River became known as the Palouse Country; colourful horses bred there were called *Palouse* horses; hence a *Palouse : Apalouse : Apalousie : Appaloosa*. The picture shows a good light-coloured *Appaloosa* at a rodeo.

UNITED STATES

Palomino

Locality: All over the United States.

Colour and characteristics: Body coat colour is that of a newly minted gold coin; mane and tail are white with not more than approximately 15 per cent dark, sorrel or chestnut hair in either; body markings free from stains or infections of smudge or smut, and free of white spots or of a distinct dorsal stripe or zebra stripes. May have white markings on the face, or white socks or stockings. The skin colour basically dark; the eyes dark. Conformation may be *Quarter Bred, Tennessee Walking Horse, Arabian, Morgan,* etc. In Great Britain the favoured type is often an *Arab-Welsh Pony* cross.

Height: Varies from about 14·2 to 15·3 h.h.

Weight: Varies from about 1,100 to 1,350 lbs.

The first *Palomino* registry was founded privately by Dick Halliday in 1932. In 1941 the Association of Palomino Horse Breeders of America was founded in California and in 1946 in Texas. The original purpose provides for the registration, purity of blood and improvement in the breeding of *Palomino* horses. In 1942 the board of directors representing twelve states voted that 'no horse should be considered if he shows coarse, draft horse, Shetland or Paint breeding'. The Association insists, after more than twenty-two years, that the horse is not yet a breed from the standpoint of breeding true, but if breeders have the wisdom to use the information available it is hoped that the next twenty years will see the goal in sight. The pictures on this page show a champion *Palomino,* Mack's Wonder Boy, with his elaborate saddlery, and a stable of fine *Palominos.*

Another champion *Palomino,* Ginn's Golden Morn.

Cow ponies in California are broken with a hackamore, the bit being used later. They are always ridden with a loose rein, since changes in pace or direction are given by moving the weight of the body in the stirrups or by a touch of the rein on the neck. One of the most famous *Palomino* sires was Old Fred, who stood 16 h.h. and weighed 1,400 lbs. Other famous sires were Sappho, Del Rey, El Rey de los Reys, and Don Julian.

Albino

The *Albino* horse is a colour type, and has been developed since 1937 by the American Albino Horse Club. A horse called Old King is considered to have been the foundation sire; he was foaled in 1906 and may have been of *Arabian-Morgan* stock. The horses are popular for circuses and parades and can, of course, be bred for riding or draught. They are of a gentle, intelligent disposition, and are claimed to be very prepotent producing beautiful all-white foals from coloured mares.

Locality: U.S.A.

Colour and characteristics: Snow white with dark eyes. Oriental characteristics and conformation, full white mane and tail. Any height.

American Percheron

Locality: United States and Canada.

Colour and characteristics: Black and grey; other colours are not popular with American breeders. These horses are noted for extra heavy muscling in the lower thighs and for an aspect of unusual ruggedness and power; fairly long croup with a big, round hip; close coupled and wide and deep through chest; plenty of back rib; the muscles of the arms, forearms, croup and gaskins are especially emphasized in a good draught horse with good legs and feet. Head and neck are typical of attractive draught horse character; full, prominent eye; broad, full forehead; straight face, strong jaw and refined ears. Clean action, ease and balance of gait are essential; markedly tractable and intelligent and an easy keeper. Sires should have a ruggedness about the head; mares feminine refinement.

Height: Stallions 16 to 17 h.h.; mares 15 to 16 h.h.

Weight: Stallions 1,800 to 2,000 lbs; mares 1,500 to 1,600 lbs.

The first *Percherons* arrived in the United States in 1839. They were sent by Edward Harris of Morristown, New Jersey. The 1880's were years of remarkable expansion for the *Percheron* business, and some of the foremost blood lines were founded. The introduction of the famous Brilliant, 1899, and his son, Brilliant, into the American stud at this time has influenced the perfection of the breed almost as much as any other event. Other important sires were Calypso, Carnot, Dragon, Laet, Lagos, Hesitation and Don Degas. Here are Lady Roxy and her stallion foal, owned by Oscar Crowell, Riverside, California.

246

American Belgian

Locality: A number of States, including Iowa, Ohio, Michigan and Indiana.

Colour and characteristics: Generally sorrel or roan, white mane and tail, white blaze on face, light points. Good, even conformation, powerful and heavy muscled; good action; friendly disposition. Used by loggers, ranchers, farmers; also popular exhibits at fairs, expositions and parades.

Height: 16 to 19 h.h. **Weight:** 1,500 to 2,000 lbs.

Although not as well-established as the *American Percheron*, which has been in the country for over a hundred years, the *American Belgian Draught Horse* is a familiar sight in a number of States, particularly in the agricultural areas. The photograph is of a typical *American Belgian* harnessed to a two-wheeled cart, at a show in Iowa.

247

American Clydesdale

Locality: Indiana, Illinois, Wisconsin, Iowa, Missouri, Minnesota and some other States.

Colour and characteristics: As for *Clydesdales* bred in Great Britain. These horses were imported into the United States in 1879 and have always been popular for transport use in teams or hitches. *Clydesdales* are also widely used in Canada as working horses or for cross-breeding.

Height: About 16·2 h.h.

An eight-horse *American Clydesdale* hitch. A team of heavy horses drawing well is capable of moving very heavy loads. 'Weight to move weight' used to be the slogan, and for short distances—and for full value for advertisement purposes—a team of four or a hitch of eight *Clydesdales* will be more economical and certainly far more effective than any motor vehicle. Heavy horses are invaluable for logging in forest areas where a tractor or lorry might become stuck, and in very wet weather.

CANADA

Royal Canadian Mounted Police Horse

Locality: Canada – Fort Walsh.

Colour and characteristics: Black or brown. A first-class saddle horse of the remount type.

Height: 15·3 to 16·3 h.h., weighing 1100 to 1250 lbs.

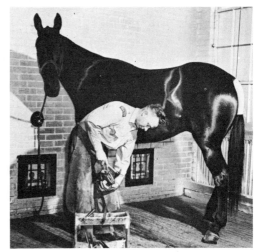

The Royal Canadian Mounted Police was originally formed (as the North-West Mounted Police) to keep order in the vast expanses of the North-West, when horses were the only means of helping the police to 'get their man'. Police horses are bred today at the stud at Fort Walsh, founded in 1940 by Commissioner S. T. Wood, from *Thoroughbred* stallions and half-bred or heavy mares. The horses are well-made with short backs and good width in the hind quarters, and they must be black or brown in colour. Every year about 500 young men enter the R.C.M.P. and equitation is considered to be an essential part of their training.

249

Locality: Canada – Sable Island, off the coast of Nova Scotia.

Colour and characteristics: Often dark chestnut, bay, brown, grey and black. Small and wiry, showing quality. Used for draught and saddle.

Height: About 14 h.h.

Sable Island Pony

There are between 275 and 300 ponies running in a wild state on Sable Island, which lies out in the Atlantic off Nova Scotia. These *Sable Island* ponies are the descendants of New England stock which was placed there early in the 18th century. While most of them are described as 'scrub', the occasional fine looking specimen occurs and the colour is often dark chestnut. They are divided into small herds, one stallion to about six to eight mares, and live without shelter all the year round, eating snow in winter for water, or breaking the ice on the fresh water pools which abound on the island. There are no trees and the ponies are dependant upon the scrub grass growing out of the island's silver sand.

250

Canadian Cutting Horse

Locality: Canada.
Colour and characteristics: Approximately the same as the American *Quarter Horse* from which it was developed (see p. 218). Can be almost any colour.
Height: 15·2 to 16·1 h.h.

Here is a *Canadian Cutting Horse* photographed at the Royal Windsor Horse Show, where they gave a display demonstrating their remarkable intelligence and training in rounding up cattle, for which the Cutting Horse has been specially developed.

251

Native Mexican

Locality: Mexico.

Colour and characteristics: Any colour. General purpose saddle pony
of apparently different types: *Spanish, Arab, Criollo*.

Height: About 15 h.h.

Undoubtedly the *Mexican* horse is, like practically all other South American horses,
a descendant of those left behind by Cortés in the 16th century. It is also more than
probable that some of its ancestors came from the American prairies, since domesticated horses went wild during several periods of the North American wars over the
centuries.

252

SOUTH AMERICA

PERU. Criollo (Costeño); Morochuco.

ARGENTINA. Criollo.

BRAZIL. Crioulo; Campolino; Mangalarga.

VENEZUELA. Llanero (Prairie) Horse.

HAITI. Haiti Pony.

SOUTH AMERICA

South America is the southern portion of a continental mass lying between the Pacific and the Atlantic Oceans, joined to the northern portion by the isthmus of Panama. There are ten republics: Brazil, Argentine, Venezuela, Columbia, Ecuador, Peru, Chile, Bolivia, Paraguay and Uraguay. It was via Panama and Jamaica, originally brought by the Conquistadores, that horses spread to all these countries.

PERU

This is an ideal country for raising superior saddle horses. As early as 1583 there were considerable herds on the ranches, including about 4,000 brood mares, and they were equal to the best in Spain. The Peruvian horse helped to populate a number of the other states. Great care was taken in breeding and there are today three recognised breeds which have changed considerably from those which the Spaniards brought with them—the *Costeño,* a first-class saddle horse, the *Chola,* a ranch horse, and the *Morochuco,* a tough, small mountain horse found in the Andes. (See pp. 256-257).

CHILE AND ARGENTINE

From Chile, which possesses the *Caballo Chileno,* the march of Spanish civilisation brought horses to the Argentine. When Pedro de Mendoza, who founded Buenos Aires in 1535, had to abandon it, he is said to have left a few horses behind. Perhaps these were joined by wild horses from Chile and Peru, because some forty years later large numbers of wild horses were to be found on the pampas.

'The Argentine mustang was of medium size with large head, thick legs, fairly prominent ears, and a big neck'.* These horses were the progenitors of the *Criollo,* one of the hardiest breeds of horses to be found in any part of the world—and one that is found in most South American republics in much the same shape and form, whether it is the *Criollo,* much-loved by the gauchos of Brazil and Uruguay, the *Llanero* or prairie horse of Venezuela, or any other of the present-day well-bred range horses.

Criollo horses appear in a variety of coat colours, such as gateado (the most popular dun-coloured with dorsal stripe and dark points); rosillo: strawberry roan; rosillo colorado: red roan; lobuno: wolf-coloured or blue dun; moro: blue roan; azulejo:

*Denhardt: *The Horse of the Americas.*

254

odd-coloured, blue and white; overo: mixed colours; alozan tosado; liver chestnut; nevada: snow-like spots.

It should be appreciated that throughout the centuries horses have been imported by the Dutch, the Portuguese, and again and again by the Spanish—these horses including both *Barbs* and *Arabs*. (See pp. 258-259).

BRAZIL

Brazil also breeds a *Crioulo (Criollo)* horse, which is about two inches smaller than the Argentine *Criollo*. There are two other breeds—the *Mangalarga*, a breed founded by a Portuguese *Altér* stallion about a hundred years ago, and the *Campolino*, a heavier horse more like the *Criollo*. The latter breed was founded by a half-bred *Andalusian* horse.

There are said to be around sixteen million horses in Brazil, but this number is not extraordinary when one considers that there are 3,287,842 square miles of land, and that no country on earth is so rich in natural resources. (See pp. 260-261).

VENEZUELA

Venezuela has 500,000 horses, and as the two photographs show these are much the same stamp as the *Criollo* and other Western prairie horses—and well they might be since they have the same forebears. The 'smallest' Venezuelan ranch will own about a hundred horses, as they are practically the only means of transport. The vaqueros, or cowboys, wear sandals with spurs attached to their bare heels, and when a young bullock has been caught the lasso is made firm to the horse's or mule's tail! This used to be the practice in North America, but was abandoned when the raised pommel of the saddle was found to be more practical. But the toughness of the *Llanero* horse, which often shows undeniable signs of his Spanish ancestors, may be appreciated when it is understood that he will pull an unwilling bullock along by his tail.

Indian ponies, which are so referred to throughout South America, are also descended from the early Spanish horses, but have been less carefully bred and are to some extent degenerated and therefore smaller, but being remarkably wiry they make ideal cow-ponies (See p. 262).

PERU

Locality: Peru.

Colour and characteristics: *Criollo* colours – dun, grey, sorrel, black, etc. Flat, broad face; bright, expressive eyes; fine muzzle and jaw; arched, muscular neck; long and sufficiently sloping shoulders; large chest; clean, short cannons; short pasterns; strong, small, well-made hooves. Compact back and rounded ribs, rounded quarters, long fine-haired tail, well placed. Thin skin covered with short fine shiny hair. The *Costeño* is valued for its easy gait, which appears to be similar to an extended pace: *paso llano, entre paso* and *agulillo*.

Height: 13·3 to 14·3 h.h.

Weight: 750-950 lbs.

Criollo (Costeño)

Horses were brought to this country by Pizarro in 1532, and today the Peruvian *Criollo* is a well-defined breed, although terrain, climate and nutrition have caused certain modifications. The *Costeño* is considered the best of the three types. It is an elegant saddle horse, and much importance is attached to his style and the smoothness of his gait, which he can maintain for long distances at different speeds. *Above* is an elegant *Criollo (Costeño)* horse.

The *Morochuco* has similar attributes to the *Costeño*. He is excellent for work in the hills and, being a good stock horse, is therefore used on many ranches throughout Peru.

A champion *Criollo* belonging to Sr. F. Peshiera.

Morochuco

Locality: Peru – The 'Serrana': high altitude.

Colour and characteristics: The forehead sometimes projects round the eyes; small ears; heavier and and shorter neck; coarser skin and generally a more angular conformation than the *Costeño*. Strong and quiet.

Height: 13·3 to 14·3 h.h.

257

Criollo

Locality: South America –
Particularly Argentine, Brazil,
Uruguay, Peru and Chile
(called *Chileno*).

Colour and characteristics:
Preferred colours are grullo, dun,
palomino, sorrel with dorsal
stripe. Head should be short and
pyramid shaped; muscular
withers; short, straight back;
large shoulders and croup;
strong legs, with short cannon
bone.

Height: 13·3 to 15 h.h.

Reconocido del Oeste *(below),* champion *Criollo* at the 1963 Palermo Show, is typical of the type that Argentinian breeders are looking for. These very strong, stocky horses are capable of great endurance, resistance to climate and fatigue. Resistance marches are frequently organised to test the *Criollos*' quality and stamina. The marches cover enormous distances, generally last eight days, and at the end the horses are raced at speed over a distance of 50 kilometres—30 miles.

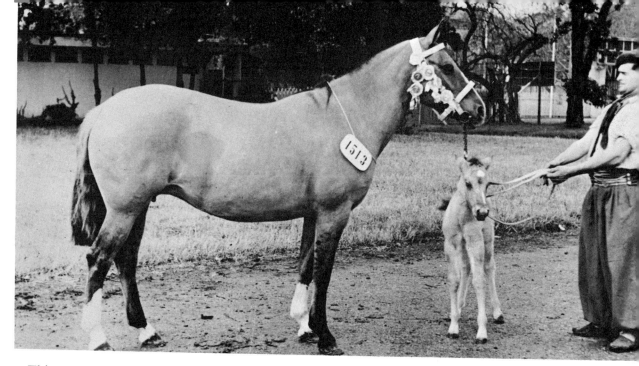

This mare and foal are particularly interesting. The mare is the favoured dun colour with the dark wither mark and zebra stripes on the legs, which may be clearly seen.

The *Criollo* 'caballo de soldado' and 'caballo de peon' are today one and the same. Mounted regiments usually prefer larger and taller horses for riding; the only regiments which may be said to make full use of the pure *Criollo* are those stationed in the arid mountainous regions of the north-west. This dun horse, a very fine type, was presented to the Granaderos a Caballo Regiment for the Rio Bamba Squadron.

Crioulo

Locality: Brazil–Sao Paulo.

Colour and characteristics: The lighter *Crioulo* colours, including bay.
The withers are more prominent and the tail is set higher; a neat head;
refined neck, but not deep through the chest. The best gait is the trot.

Height: 14·3½ h.h.

The fourth largest country in the world has three breeds of horses: the *Crioulo* of
Rio Grande de Sul, the *Mangalarga* and the *Campolino*. All are descendants of the
South American *Criollo* (Portuguese *Crioulo*). Over one hundred years ago the
Emperor Peter II of Brazil imported the *Altér* stallion (see p. 255) Sublime and the
resultant breeding in the succeeding century shows a definite reversion towards the
Barb type. Our photograph shows Pilcomayo ridden by Lt. Moreira of the Andrade
Neves Regiment.

260

Campolino

and

Mangalarga

Locality: Brazil – Meiras Gerais.

Colour and characteristics:
Grey, sorrel, roan, bay, etc. The
two breeds are similar, but the
Campolino has short pasterns, and
shorter cannon bone and a deeper
chest than the *Mangalarga.*

Height: About 14·3 h.h.

The *Campolino* is considered to be a heavier horse suitable for saddle and draught.
Sr. Cassiano Campolino founded this breed a century ago. Here again, a part-
Andalusian stallion, Monarcha, was used on the *Crioulo.*

261

Llanero

Locality: Venezuela.

Colour and characteristics: Dun, yellow with black or dark mane and tail, white spotted brown and black mane and tail, white and yellow/cream 'Pinto'; other colours. The Venezuelan *Criollo* appears to be a lighter type, with finer limbs, than the Argentine *Criollo*.

Height: Not over 15·2 h.h.

Horses were brought to the Americas by the Spanish during the 16th century and today the *Llanero* or Prairie Horses have pride of place. Venezuela alone has an estimated 500,000 horses, which are kept in herds, used by cowboys or employed as the normal means of transport. They still closely resemble the *Barb* and *Andalusian*, both in conformation (particularly the head) and colour—yellow with black or dark mane and tail; white spotted brown and black mane and tail; or, like the dappled stallion, Motilon *(right)*, white and yellow.

262

Haiti Pony

Locality: Haiti.

Colour and characteristics: Any colour, browns and blacks prevailing.
Conformation that of an all-round useful pony with some Oriental blood.
Very hardy and sure-footed.

Height: About 14 h.h.

These *Haiti* ponies cannot be described as a breed. Very little information is available about them, but without any doubt they would have been imported, very probably from North and South America. There are about 150 ponies available to carry cruise passengers to Sans-Souci Palace and the Citadel Henri Christophe, in the northern part of the island of Haiti. The journey takes four hours and the ponies have to be surefooted as the going is very rocky.

263

CONCLUSION

On the foregoing pages the many breeds and types of horses and ponies have been traced across the surface of the globe. The photographs have taken us to lands of which many have dreamed and with which others are familiar; some of the horses and their accoutrements represent cultures and civilisations several thousands of years old, and if the stories of these could be told they would fill many volumes.

We have seen how the horse has conquered continents and how he is today still the valued friend of man whom he serves as no other animal on earth has ever done.

A careful study of the photographs will show how points of conformation have been passed from one breed to another, how desired characteristics have been 'handed on'. Little known, unknown and world famous breeds have been presented to the reader that he or she may gain pleasure and profit therefrom.

Horses are living creatures with the positive feelings known to all of us, but one thing they do not share with us is the mischievousness with which mankind has been cursed. We have had the world at our feet: the mist-covered valleys, the forests, the mountains and moorlands, the vast steppes and pampas and the hot dry deserts; the islands, countries and continents where diverse languages, ideas and misunderstandings divide mankind, save for one thing—horses—and where there is appreciation of a good horse, there is a bond common to us all.

BIBLIOGRAPHY

R. M. Denhardt: *The Horse of the Americas*

Miss F. M. Prior: Article, 'The Racehorse'

Dr. George Gaylord Simpson: *Horses*

Tom Ryder: *The High Stepper*

R. S. Summerhays: *Encyclopaedia for Horsemen*

R. S. Summerhays: *Observer's Book of Horses and Ponies*

Walker D. Wyman: *The Wild Horse of the West*

Xenophon: *The Art of Horsemanship* (trans: M. H. Morgan)

Dr. Frances Haines: *Appaloosa: The Spotted Horse in Art and History*

John Patten: *The Light Horse Breeds*

Prof. J. A. Gorman: *The Western Horse*

A. M. Boden and Max Wimmer: *Hippologisches Lexicon*

Dr. Bruno Deschamps: *Über Pferde*

Dr. Johannes Erich Flade: *Das Araberpferd*

Sir John Hammond, Prof. Dr. I. Johansson, Prof. D. F. Haring: *Handbuch der Tierzüchtung: Rassen Kunde,* Vol. 3

H. Neuschulz: *Pferdezucht*

Dr. Erna Mohr: *Das Urwildpferd*

Baroness van Heemstra: *Het Friese Paard*

Dr. Zdenek Veselovsky: *Equus*

Prof. Dr. Zorn: *Pferdezucht*

Dr. Franz Hancar: *Das Pferd in Prähistorischer und Früher Historischer Zeit*

Dr. Withold Pruski and Magdalena Jaworowska: *Roczniki Nauk Rolniczych* (The Works and Studies conducted in Poland on Regeneration of Wild Horses called Tarpans)

Dr. Withold Pruski: *Rocznikli Nauk Rolniczych* (Wild Horses of Eastern Europe)

Author: *Die Pferde mit der Elchschaufel*

S. Ruy d'Andrade: *Alrededor del Caballo Español: O Cavallo do Sorraia; Garranos: La Crises del Caballo Andaluz*

Henry Aubanel: *Les Chevaux Blancs du Camargue*

Literature provided by most of the Breed Societies

INDEX

Numbers in parenthesis indicate pages on which illustrations appear

267